The Euthanasia Controversy

1812–1974

The Euthanasia Controversy

1812–1974

A Bibliography with Select Annotations

by

Charles W. Triche III

and

Diane Samson Triche

The Whitston Publishing Company
Troy, New York
1975

Copyright 1975
Charles W. Triche III
Diane Samson Triche

Library of Congress Catalog Card Number 75-8379
ISBN 0-87875-071-1

Printed in the United States of America

FOR: CHARLES WALTER

PREFACE

Arguments for and against euthanasia, both active and passive, are currently gaining increasing world-wide attention. Doctors are no longer the only individuals concerned in an active way with the subject or the problem. Lawyers, clergy, and laymen alike have begun to voice their opinions concerning the topic. The literature regarding euthanasia has been increasing in great proportions. As a result of this increase and because of a felt need for a complete bibliography on the subject of euthanasia, this present work has been compiled.

While compiling this near complete selectively annotated bibliography, over thirty indexing and abstracting services have been consulted, as well as bibliographies appearing in monographs and serial publications. It would, however, be impossible to list all the sources consulted during the compilation of this bibliography. Nevertheless, some of the major sources of information should be mentioned. These sources are: THE APPLIED SCIENCE AND TECHNOLOGY INDEX, AMERICAN BOOK PUBLISHING RECORD, BIBLIOGRAPHICAL INDEX, BIOLOGICAL ABSTRACTS, BIOLOGICAL AND AGRICULTURAL INDEX, BOOKS IN PRINT: SUBJECTS, CANADIAN PERIODICALS INDEX, CHEMICAL ABSTRACTS, CUMULATIVE BOOK INDEX, CUMULATIVE INDEX TO NURSING LITERATURE, DISSERTATION ABSTRACTS, EDUCATION INDEX, ERIC, ESSAY AND GENERAL LITERATURE INDEX, HOSPITAL LITERATURE INDEX, INDEX ANALYTIQUE, INDEX MEDICUS, INDEX TO CANADIAN LEGAL PERIODICALS, INDEX TO LEGAL PERIODICALS, NATIONAL OBSERVER INDEX, NEW YORK TIMES INDEX, LIBRARY OF CONGRESS CATALOG: BOOKS: SUBJECTS, PUBLIC AFFAIRS INFORMATION SERVICE, POOLE'S INDEX TO PERIODICAL LITERATURE, READER'S GUIDE TO PERIODICAL LITERATURE, SOCIAL SCIENCES AND HUMANITIES INDEX (also: SOCIAL SCIENCES INDEX and HUMANITIES INDEX when these divided·), and SOCIOLOGICAL ABSTRACTS.

This bibliography is a selected, annotated bibliography. The annotations contained within the work are not intended to serve as a substitute for the original article. The purpose of the annotation is to provide enough information on the content of the book or article analyzed to allow the researcher to determine whether or not he wishes to consult the work for additional information. In most instances, no qualitative judgments have been made on the relative merit of the individual works listed. Nevertheless, where a work has been of particular significance, such significance has been noted within the annotation.

The bibliography is divided into three main sections. These sections are: Section 1: Books and Essays; Section 2: Subject Index to Periodical Literature; and Section 3: Author Index.

In the "Books and Essays" section, books, essays, and pamphlets are listed alphabetically by author when an author has been listed. Anonymous works are listed within the same alphabet by title. General annotations for major books on the subject of euthanasia have been abbreviated, the reason for this being that analytics and annotations for each of the chapters, sections or essays contained within the work have been provided.

The arrangement of the "Subject Index to Periodical Literature" is alphabetical by title within each subject heading. However, there exists one exception to this generalization. In the subject section "Cases of Mercy Killings", quite naturally an abundance of newspaper articles appear. Periodical literature coverage for this section is arranged alphabetically by title and listed before the specific case's newspaper coverage. The newspaper material has been arranged chronologically so that the researcher can place the public's reaction,

progress of the case, and the subsequent
outcome of the case in proper perspective.

In instances where the material contained
in an article crosses disciplines or pertinent
schools of thought, the material has been re-
peated in each section to which the material
relates. However, when the material in one
section largely overlaps material in another
section of this bibliography, the researcher
is referred to additional subject headings within the bibliography through a SEE ALSO cross
reference.

This bibliography is a numbered bibliography; therefore, the numbers appearing after
the names of individuals within the author
index refer to the bibliographic citation numbers and not to specific pages within the book.

No abbreviations appear in this bibliography. Complete journal titles and languages
are given. The original language in which a
particular article is written has been provided
in most cases. Also, a list of languages in
which translations or summaries are available
has been included at the end of the bibliographic entry when this information has been
available.

We find it quite impossible to thank or
acknowledge all the individuals who have assisted
us during the compilation of this bibliography.
We would like to mention and thank several persons who have been of particular help. We do
thank J. W. Gordon Gourlay, Director of the
Clemson University Library, for his encourage-
ment and assistance in calling to our attention
new books on the subject of euthanasia. Also,
Marian H. Withington, Della Gale Campbell,
Genevieve L. Reidy and Peggy Cover must be thanked
for their professional advice and assistance.
And we would like to acknowledge the technical
assistance of Rita Schubert and Miriam Mitchell,

who gathered much of the material so that it
could be annotated.

CWT
DST
Clemson, S. C.
February 22, 1975

LITERATURE ANALYSIS

Euthanasia is a very difficult word to define because it has attracted so much emotive terminology and ambiguity. In many of the articles in our book, and with increasing public usage, the word, euthanasia, has been used synonymously with the words, "mercy killing". However, many persons violently object to this general misnomer.

We the compilers, had difficulty in choosing a word that could best describe the literature, when that literature uses the word euthanasia indiscriminately for both easy death and mercy killing. Therefore, when we entitle this work, The Euthanasia Controversy, we are including all topics dealing with euthanasia and its various connotations; however, we recognize the differences.

Euthanasia, as an act of mercy, has been divided or categorized into two basic forms: active euthanasia and passive euthanasia. Many proponents of euthanasia programs make fine distinctions between these two forms. Under the subject heading "General: For Euthanasia", the researcher may find arguments supporting all forms of euthanasia. Usually these arguments are structured forms of passive euthanasia--omitting treatment or withholding extraordinary measures.

Active euthanasia is most often defined as a direct act (used synonymously with the terms positive or direct euthanasia) whereby an individual takes measures to end the life of a suffering, incurable, or mentally incompetent individual. The term active applies when an individual dies from the results of an event other than the event of his illness. The death occurs by external measures directly applied.

One form of active euthanasia which causes particular controversy is that form which has

been termed "aided suicide", a form of death
help. In sections "General Periodical Literature", "General: For Euthanasia", and "Suicide",
the researcher may find assertions made that
suicide is an inherent right of man, and that
individuals have or have not the right to choose
their time to die. One form of aided suicide
which might be of particular interest is that
form discussed through an analysis of Eskimo
culture.

Passive euthanasia is often defined as a
lack of action taken (frequently termed indirect
or negative euthanasia) on the part of the physician or layman in the treatment of the terminally ill patient. Passive forms of euthanasia
vary from omissions of treatment or withholding
treatment, to a refusal on the part of the patient to allow treatment to be administered.
The passive euthanasia enthusiast's argument
often centers around the ethics of not prolonging a person's suffering and emphasis is placed
on the maintenance of a quality of existence.
Individuals arguing for passive euthanasia, as
do the active euthanasia proponents, argue for
a sense of ethics in the treatment of the
terminally ill patient.

Euthanasia can present a moral dilemma.
The clergy have not been able to resolve the
controversy from doctrinal or theological viewpoints. In the "Morality of Euthanasia" and
"Decisions and Medical Ethics" sections, the
researcher will find arguments weighted toward
both support and rejection of euthanasia. However, both clergy and physician argue for a
standardization of guidelines for the treatment of the terminally ill patients.

Currently, the act of euthanasia has
many legal consequences; therefore, much of
the literature surrounding the subject includes
a discussion of euthanasia's legal implications.
This bibliography contains a wealth of material

which examines the legal ramifications of active
and passive euthanasia, the withdrawal of extraordinary means, the implications of the decision
not to resuscitate, aided suicide, and the present legal status of euthanasia. "The Law and
Euthanasia" section additionally contains information relating the history of the euthanasia
movement, and an analysis of euthanasia from
the mid-nineteenth century to the present. Legislation in the United States (including the
State Legislative action of Ohio, New York, New
Jersey and Florida) and Great Britain is examined
in detail.

Resolution of the euthanasia controversy
does not seem possible in the near future. Euthanasia has, nevertheless, been given more attention and serious thought. And perhaps such
serious consideration will lead to an equitable
solution.

TABLE OF CONTENTS

BOOKS AND ESSAYS

1 Alexander, L. "Science under dictatorship,"
  NEW YORK ACADEMY OF MEDICINE. FUTURE IN
  MEDICINE. New York: Columbia University
  Press, 1951. pp. 51-106

2 Alsop, Stewart. STAY OF EXECUTION: A SORT OF
  MEMOIR. Philadelphia: Lippincott, 1973.
    A personal narrative of a fight against
  leukemia by a terminally ill journalist.

3 Barrere,,Igor. LE DOSSIER CONFIDENTIEL DE
  L'EUTHANASIE. Paris: Stock, 1962.

4 Barrington, Mary Rose. "Apologia for
  suicide," EUTHANASIA AND THE RIGHT TO DEATH:
  THE CASE FOR VOLUNTARY EUTHANASIA. (Gould)
  London: Peter Owen, 1970. pp. 152-172.
    Options for the individual's right to
  select the time and circumstances for the
  termination of his existence. Examines
  prior and current beliefs and suggests that
  the individual's final gift is death.
  "...If we can bring ourselves to chose our
  time for acceptance, so much the better for
  us ... and for society."

5 Beels, C. Christian. "The ceremony of dying,"
  THE RIGHT TO DIE: DECISION AND DECISION
  MAKERS. New York: Jason Aronson, 1970.
    Suggests that death be placed in social
  perspective. Death, as a social matter,
  requires the interrelationships of patient,
  physician, family and clergy.

6 Benoliel, Jeanne. DEALING WITH DEATH. Los
  Angelos, University of Southern California:
  Ethel Percy Adams Gerontology Center, 1973.
    Discussions of death presented for those
  concerned with the delivery of care service
  for the elderly.

7 Blanshard, Paul. AMERICAN FREEDOM AND CATHOLIC
  POWER. New York: Holt, Rinehart and Winston,
  1964.
    Reviews the doctrinal attitudes of the

Catholic Church concerning controversial
issues. Specific coverage is given to the
Catholic Church in the United States.

8 Blomquist, Clarence. LIVET DODEN OCH
   LAKAREN: OM MEDICINSK DODSHJALP. Uddervalls,
   Sweden: Zinderman, 1964. (Swedish)

9 Bloom, Samuel W. THE DOCTOR AND HIS PATIENT:
   A SOCIOLOGICAL STUDY. New York: The Free
   Press, 1965.
      Suggests that the physician should maintain
   an affective neutrality in some situations.
   Illustrates the point with a case involving
   euthanasia.

10 Bok, Sissela Ann. VOLUNTARY EUTHANASIA.
   Cambridge, Mass.: Harvard University
   Graduate School, 1970. (PhD Dissertation)

11 Butler, Robert N. "The personal sense and the
   social structure of legacy: an ethic to
   the future," THE RIGHT TO DIE: DECISION
   AND DECISION MAKERS. New York: Jason
   Aronson, 1974. pp. 27-41.
      Discusses the individual's feelings
   concerning his sense of progeny and his
   deep personal sense to leave something
   constructive of oneself. The purpose of
   the article is the development of a
   sensibility and of social support for an
   ethic to the future which will help
   people die and will help their survivors
   as well.

12 CIBA Foundation Synposium. Ethics in Medical
   Progress, London, 1966. ETHICS IN MEDICAL
   PROGRESS. Ciba Foundation, 1966.
      Extraordinary measures are discussed
   as well as replies to Pope Pius XII's
   views on reanimation presented.

13 Cameron, D. C. S. THE TRUTH ABOUT CANCER.
   Englewood Cliffs, N. J.: Prentice-Hall,
   1956.
      Discusses the difference between eutha-
   nasia and allowing a patient to die.

2

14   Campbell, Alastair V.   MORAL DILEMMAS IN
     MEDICINE. London: Churchill Livingston,
     1972.   pp. 36, 91, 94-97, 100-104, 173-
     185.
        Considers the concerns of doctors and
     nurses as they relate to their sense of
     responsibility for the health and welfare
     of modern society. Considers the indi-
     vidual and his decisions as well as per-
     mitting death, resuscitation, withholding
     treatment, switching off machines, ethical
     considerations, pain killing and respect
     for life.

15   "The care of the incurable and the dying,"
     YOUR DEATH WARRANT: THE IMPLICATIONS
     OF EUTHANASIA. (Gould) London: Chap-
     man, 1971. pp. 89-96.
        Portrays the role of the doctor as
     one of avoiding treatment for treatment's
     sake or for the sake of devotion to the
     professional expertise when this treat-
     ment serves no useful purpose save the
     prolongation of the patient's pain and
     suffering with no hope of a meaningful
     recovery.

16   Carlisle, Anthony. AN ESSAY ON THE DIS-
     ORDERS OF OLD AGE AND ON THE MEANS OF
     PROLONGING HUMAN LIFE. London: Longman,
     Hurst, Ries, Orme and Brown, 1818.
        Comments on the physicians' role in
     treating the dying patient. Includes
     arguments for the prolongation of human life.
     Of particular interest are pages 12-13,
     100, 109 and 110 where medical judgment
     and physicians' obligations are treated in
     detail. From a historical viewpoint, the
     work presents many of the ageless argu-
     ments used today for the prolonging of
     life and for the refusing of active eutha-
     nasia.

17   Catel, W. BORDERLINE SITUATIONS OF LIFE.
     Nuremberg, 1962.

18   Catel, Werner. GREZSITUATIONEN ZUM PROBLEM

3

EUTHANASIE. Nurnberg: Glock un. Lutz,
1962. (German)

19 Catel, Werner. LIEDMINDERUNG RIGHTIE
VERSTANDEN MIT EINER EINLEITUNG VON FABIAN
VON SCHIABRENDORFF. Nurnberg: Glock u.
Lutz, 1966. (German)

20 Challaye, Jean. MEDECINE ET EUTHANASIE.
Paris: Universite Paris, 1945. (Thesis)
(French)

21 Charles, Raymond. PEUT-ON ADMETTRE L'
EUTHANASIA. PARES ENSEIGNEMENT ET PERFECT-
IONNEMENT TECHNIQUES. Librarie de Journal
des Notaires et de Avocats, 1955.

22 Church of England. Board of Social
Responsibility. DECISIONS ABOUT LIFE AND
DEATH: A PROBLEM IN MODERN MEDICINE.
London: Church Information Office, 1965.

23 Cuello, Calon Eugenio. TRES TEMAS PENALES:
EL ABORTO CRIMINAL EL PROBLEMS PENAL DE LA
EUTANASIA, EL ASPECTO PENAL DE LA FECUNDA-
CION ARTIFICIAL. Barcelona: Bosh, 1955.

24 Curran, Charles E. MEDICINE AND MORALS.
Washington: Corpus Books, 1970.

25 Dedek, John F. "Euthanasia," HUMAN LIFE:
SOME MORAL ISSUES. New York: Sheed and
Ward, 1972. pp. 119-142.
   Presents a general review of the topic
during which human attitudes toward death
are discerned. Discusses theological
views, especially Catholic views, and
defines active euthanasia.

26 Donnelly, John. "The physician as an instru-
ment in bringing death," THE RIGHT TO DIE:
DECISION AND DECISION MAKERS. New York:
Jason Aronson, 1974. pp. 68-70.
   Comments briefly on the issue of death by
suicide and on death by patient requesting

that he be allowed to die.

27   Downing, A. B. (ed.) EUTHANASIA AND THE
      RIGHT TO DEATH: THE CASE FOR VOLUNTARY
      EUTHANASIA. London: Peter Owens,1969.
      Also published by: Humanities Press,
      1970 and by Nash Publishing Corporation,
      1970.
          The essays summarize the question:
      "Is it a human right for an individual
      to be allowed to choose for himself the
      merciful release of death?" Voluntary
      Euthanasia Bill, memorandum, text and
      schedule included in appendix.

28   Downing, A. B. "Euthanasia: the human
      context," EUTHANASIA AND THE RIGHT TO
      DEATH: THE CASE FOR VOLUNTARY EUTHANASIA.
      (Downing) London: Peter Owens, 1969,
      pp. 13-24.

          Seeks to define the role of the physician
      in humane treatment of patients pointing
      out instances where kindness can be cruelty.

29   Dublin, L. I. and M. Spiegelman. LENGTH OF
      LIFE. New York: Ronald Press, 1949.

30   Ehrhardt, Helmut. EUTHANASIE UND VERNICHTUNG
      'LEBENSIENIWERTEN' LEBENS MIT EINEM VORWORT
      VON HAND HOFF. Stuttgart: F. Enke, 1965.
      (German)

31   Eisenberg, John. THE RIGHT TO LIVE AND DIE:
      CANADIAN CRITICAL ISSUES. Toronto:
      Ontario Institute for Studies in Education,
      1973.

          Conflicts from issues arising over
      counterclaims to the control of birth,
      life and death are raised. Cases of mercy
      killings, religious views and medical views
      are presented. An analysis of the problems
      presented by the issues of euthanasia,
      abortion, capital punishment, etc. follows
      with information that renders proper per-
      spectives to these issues.

32   Eissler, K. R. THE PSYCHIATRIST AND THE DYING
          PATIENT. New York: International Univ-
          ersities Press, 1955.
          Asserts the patient's role in the dying
      process is one which leads to happiness
      along the "terminal pathway". Suggests
      that drastic measures may hinder this
      peaceful transition.

33   Elliott, Neil. THE GODS OF LIFE. New
          York: Macmillan, 1974.
          Discusses medical care of the aged in
      the United States, types of terminal
      care and euthanasia and its medical ethics.
      Includes bibliographical references.

34   "The ethics of euthanasia," YOUR DEATH
          WARRANT: THE IMPLICATIONS OF EUTHANASIA.
          (Gould) London: Chapman, 1971. pp.
          79-88.
          Seeks to define aspects of euthanasia
      which would be acceptable to those who
      do not subscribe to a formal faith.
      Many arguments are drawn from traditional
      Christian Doctrine.

35   The Euthanasia Society. BULLETIN, v. 1-
          October, 1947-   . New York:
          Euthanasia Society of America.

36   Euthanasia Society. London. THE CASE
          FOR VOLUNTARY EUTHANASIA. London:
          Euthanasia Society, 1961.
          The Euthanasia Society of London
      presents a case for voluntary euthanasia
      which would permit an adult of sound mind
      to choose between an easy death and a
      hard one with medical aid in implement-
      ing that choice.

37   "Euthanasia, the family and society,"
          YOUR DEATH WARRANT: THE IMPLICATIONS
          OF EUTHANASIA. (Gould) London: Chapman,
          1971. pp. 122-129.
          Considers pro-euthanasia arguments not
      only in terms of compassion for the dying

person, but also in terms of the relatives and friends involved and intimately associated with the death.

38 DIE EUTHANASIE: BEITRAGE von STEPHEN DIXON et al. Hrsg. von Fritz Valentin. Gottigen, Vandenhoeck and Ruprecht, 1969.

39 Fisher, Jochen. EUTHANASIE HEUTE? Munchen: Kaiser, 1968. (German)

40 Fletcher, George P. "Prolonging life: some legal considerations," EUTHANASIA AND THE RIGHT TO DEATH: THE CASE FOR VOLUNTARY EUTHANASIA. (Downing) London: Peter Owen, 1970. pp. 71-84.
    Examines the traditional attitudes of the legal and medical profession to death. Creates arguments around evidence that common law courts have never convicted a practitioner for refusing sustaining aid to a terminal patient.

41 Fletcher, Joseph. "Euthanasia and Anti-dysthanasia," MORAL RESPONSIBILITY. Philadelphia: Westmenster, 1967. pp. 140-160.
    Discusses direct and indirect euthanasia.

42 Fletcher, Joseph. "The patient's right to die," EUTHANASIA AND THE RIGHT TO DEATH: THE CASE FOR VOLUNTARY EUTHANASIA. (Downing) London: Peter Owen, 1970. pp. 61-70.
    The individual's right to die is examined with conditions of maintained existences analyzed. Reviews medical morals and the civil law.

43 Fletcher, Joseph F. MORALS AND MEDICINE. Princeton, New Jersey: Princeton University Press, 1965. Also published by: London: Victor Gallany, 1954.

Ltd., 1954.
Medical ethics concerning euthanasia are analyzed. Emphasis is on the patient's right to know the truth about his condition with sections on keeping the patient alive and moral responsibility included.

44 Flew, Anthony. "Is to ought," EVOLUTION-ARY ETHICS. London: Macmillan, 1967. Ch. 4.

45 Flew, Anthony. "The principle of euthanasia," EUTHANASIA AND THE RIGHT TO DEATH: THE CASE FOR VOLUNTARY EUTHANASIA. (Downing) London: Peter Owen, 1970. pp. 31-48.
Flew argues for voluntary euthanasia and the establishment of a legal right to request euthanasia. Additionally, he is concerned with the morality of the issue and with general principles such as abuse prevention, patient's wishes and euthanasia legislation.

46 Ford, J. C. MERCY MURDER. American Press, 1951. 16pp. (PAIS)

47 Gillon, Raanan. "Suicide and voluntary euthanasia: historical perspective," EUTHANASIA AND THE RIGHT TO DEATH: THE CASE FOR VOLUNTARY EUTHANASIA. (Downing) London: Peter Owen, 1970. pp. 173-193.
Differentiates between imposed or compulsory euthanasia and assisted suicide. Compares these ideas and places them in historical perspective.

48 Goppinger, Hans F. ARZT UND RECHT MEDEZINISCH-JURISTISCHE GRENZPROBLEME UNSERER ZEIT. Munchen: C. H. Beck, 1966.
Analyzes the physician's role as pertaining to the legal ramifications of medical practice.

49   Goldfarb, Alvin I. "The need for predeter-
      mined guidelines," THE RIGHT TO DIE:
      DECISION AND DECISION MAKERS. New York:
      Jason Aronson, 1974. p. 76.
        "Where there is little time to acquire
      information about the patient...we may
      benefit from socially predetermined guide-
      lines which press us to maintain life."

50   Goldfarb, Alvin I. "The preoccupation of
      society with death and dying," THE RIGHT
      TO DIE: DECISION AND DECISION MAKERS.
      New York: Jason Aronson, 1974. pp. 15-
      20.
        Discusses society's acceptance or
      rejection of the idea of death and the
      social pressures brought to bear on the
      acceptance of death.

51   Gonzalez Bustamante, Juan Jose. EUTHANASIA
      Y CULTURA. Mexico: Associacion Mexicana
      de Sociologia, 1952. (Spanish)

52   Gorney, Roderic. "A cross-cultural comparison"
      THE RIGHT TO DIE: DECISION AND DECISION
      MAKERS. New York: Jason Aronson, 1974.
      pp. 71-72
        Suggests that a better way of under-
      standing the human need and of attitudes
      toward survival of loved ones is acquired
      by studying other cultures via cross-
      cultural comparison of attitudes toward
      the dying process.

53   Gould, Jonathan (ed) YOUR DEATH WARRANT?
      THE IMPLICATIONS OF EUTHANASIA. London:
      Geoffrey Chapman, 1971. Also published by:
      Arlington House, 1973.
        Includes the history and development
      of the euthanasia movement; medical-legal
      and ethical studies. Appendix includes
      the text of the Bill introduced, House of
      Lords, March, 1969. Legislation is
      examined, 1936-1969.

54 Greenleigh, Lawrence F. "Dying-the power
    and the prize," THE RIGHT TO DIE:
    DECISION AND DECISION MAKERS. New York:
    Jason Aronson, 1974. pp. 41-49
       Examines the motivations such as relief
    from pain, protection or peace, which
    direct the individual toward a beneficient
    gain in wishing to die. Also analyzes
    the suicidal act and examines individual's
    motives for committing suicide.

55 Gresham. G. A. "A time to be born and a
    time to die," EUTHANASIA AND THE RIGHT
    TO DEATH: THE CASE FOR VOLUNTARY EUTHA-
    NASIA. (Downing) London: Peter Owen,
    1970. pp. 148-151.
       Considers the meaning of human life
    uncomplicated by the religious argument.
    Discusses the dignity of human life and
    honoring patient's wishes to die by
    acceptance of those wishes by the phy-
    sician. Uses case histories to illustrate
    his argument for a dignified death.

56 Group for the Advancement of Psychiatry.
    THE RIGHT TO DIE: DECISION AND DECISION
    MAKERS. New York: Jason Aronson, 1974.
       Analyzes the right of the individual
    to determine where and under what cir-
    cumstances he may choose to terminate his
    life. Consists of discussions, obser-
    vations and reactions to life and death
    confrontations with a selection of case
    material.

57 Hafey, E. S. E. REPRODUCTION AND BREEDING
    TECHNIQUES FOR LABORATORY ANIMALS.
    Philadelphia: Lea & Febiger, 1970.
       Contains an appendix which includes an
    analysis of the legal aspects of animal
    care specifically information concerning
    anesthesia and euthanasia.

58 Haldane, J. B. "Euthanasia," SCIENCE
    ADVANCES. Allen, 1948. pp. 176-178.

59   Haring, Bernard. MEDICAL ETHICS. Notre
      Dame, Indiana: Fides Publishers Inc.,
      1973. pp. 111, 121, 140-150.
        The major emphasis of this section
      is on definition of general terms with
      emphasis on negative euthanasia and its
      problems. Contains a section entitles:
      "No to positive euthanasia".

60   Hartl, Albert. EUTHANASIE IN RELIGIOSER
      SICHT. Hamlen: Sottsien, 1965.
        Analyzes euthanasia's relationship
      to religious doctrine.

61   Hauff, Wolfram von. EUTHANASIE; STERBEHILFE
      UND TODESLENDERUNG? Beuron: Hohenzollern
      Verlag, 1950. (German)

62   Hauser, Fritz. DIE FRAGE DER EUTHANASIE
      IM SCHWEIZERISCHEN STRAFRECHT. Zurich:
      Juris-Verlag, 1952. (German)

63   Hickey, H. EUTHANASIA. Truth Seeker, 1902.

64   Hickey, H. EUTHANASIA. Truth Seeker, 1912.

65   Hinton, John. DYING. Gretna, La.: Pelican
      Press, 1967.
        Argues that euthanasia may eliminate
      much of the torment and agony associated
      with dying.

66   "History and development of the euthanasia
      movement," YOUR DEATH WARRANT: THE
      IMPLICATIONS OF EUTHANASIA. (Gould)
      London: Chapman, 1971. pp. 20-28.
        Takes the history and development of
      the euthanasia movement through early times
      and primitive peoples through the present
      day with emphasis on its development from
      1870.

67   Holmer, S. J. "Some controversial questions
      of right and wrong," LIFE AND MORALS.
      New York: Macmillan, 1948. pp. 144-175.

68 Honolka, Bert. DIE KREIZELSCHREIBER.
    ARZTE OHNE GEWISSEN: EUTHANASIE IM
    DRITTEN REICH. Hamberg: Rutten & Loening,
    1961. (German)

69 "The human problems of euthanasia," YOUR
    DEATH WARRANT: THE IMPLICATIONS OF EUTHA-
    NASIA. (Gould) London: Chapman, 1971.
    pp. 97-106.
       The person as distinct from the principle
    of euthanasia is considered as the author
    examines the human problems which could
    have arisen had the 1969 Voluntary
    Euthanasia bill become law.

70 Iglesias Salis, Manuel. ABORTO, EUTANASIA
    Y FECUNDACION ARTIFIAL. Barcelona:
    Dux, 1954.

71 Kaplan, Abraham. "Summation," THE RIGHT
    TO DIE: DECISION AND DECISION MAKERS.
    New York: Jason Aronson, 1974. pp. 58-
    67.
       Collects and condenses views presented
    at the symposium reported here.

72 Kenyon, Carleton W. A SELECTIVE BIBLIOGRAPHY
    ON POPULATION CONTROL. Sacramento, Calif.:
    California State Library - Law Library, 1966.
    Supplement compiled by Lorna Fischer, 1969.

73 Kohl, Marvin. THE MORALITY OF KILLING:
    SANCTITY OF LIFE, ABORTION AND
    EUTHANASIA. London: Peter Owen, 1974.
    Also published by: New York: Humanities
    Press, 1974.
       Reviews the legal implications of
    euthanasia and abortion.

74 Komisar, Yale. "Euthanasia legislation:
    some non-religious objections," EUTHANASIA
    AND THE RIGHT TO DEATH: THE CASE FOR
    VOLUNTARY EUTHANASIA. (Downing) London:
    Peter Owen, 1970. pp. 85-133.
       The Law on the Books operates to stay
    the hand of all concerned. This law

includes (1) the presently incurable, (2) those beyond the aid of any respite which may come along in his life expectancy, suffering, (3) those cases which are intolerable and (4) those in unmitigable pain and a fixed and rational desire to die. Komisar argues that euthanasia progress may open the wedge for more objectionable practices.

75 Krant, Melvin J. DYING WITH DIGNITY - THE MEANING AND CONTROL OF PERSONAL DEATH. Springfield, Illinois: C. C. Thomas, 1974.
    Includes discussions of the fears about dying together with facts about dying, the indignities involved in the dying process, family-patient relationships, and an analysis of the physician's role during a fatal illness.

76 Kubler-Ross, E. ON DEATH AND DYING. New York: Macmillain, 1969.
    Describes necessary stages of development leading to adaptation to dying and death.

77 "The law and artificial prolongation of life," PAPER. Read before the Christian Education Committee. United Presbyterian Church, U. S. A. Chicago, January 12, 1967.

78 "The law and the legal implications of euthanasia," YOUR DEATH WARRANT: THE IMPLICATIONS OF EUTHANASIA. (Gould) London: Chapman, 1971. pp. 68-78.
    Begins with a treatise on the current law of homicide. Euthanasia and essential procedural requirements are defined. Examines the concepts of voluntary v/s involuntary euthanasia.

79 LAWS OF LIFE. "Euthanasia," by J. G. Sutherland. Sheed, 1936. pp. 260-270.

80 "Legislative proposals. Comments on bills and draft bills, 1936-1969," YOUR DEATH

WARRANT: THE IMPLICATIONS OF EUTHANASIA.
(Gould) London: Chapman, 1971.
pp. 29-37.
Reviews the 1936 United Kingdom
Euthanasia Bill, the Nebraska Bill of
1938, the 1968 Draft Bill and the euthanasia debate in the House of Lords in 1969.

81   Linden, Maurice E. "Immediate alternatives
      for the dying patient," THE RIGHT TO DIE:
      DECISION AND DECISION MAKERS. New York:
      Jason Aronson, 1974. pp. 54-57.
      Reports two clinical experiences with
      aging patients illustrating some of the
      problems encountered in the field of
      geriatric psychiatry.

82   MacGillivray, G. J. SUICIDE AND EUTHANASIA.
      Catholic Trust Society. n. p.
      Insists that human beings are God's
      property and not man's.

83   Maguire, Daniel. DEATH BY CHOICE. New York:
      Doubleday, 1974.
      Presents discussions on various attitudes
      toward death along with general concepts
      surrounding euthanasia. Includes biblio-
      graphical references.

84   Mannes, Marya. LAST RIGHTS. New York:
      Morrow, 1974.
      Mannes recognizes several distinctions
      made in discussions of active and
      passive euthanasia. She distinguishes
      between euthanasia and mercy killing and
      contrasts positive and negative - volun-
      tary and involuntary euthanasia.

85   Marx, Paul. O. S. B. ABORTION, EUTHANASIA:
      WHAT NEXT. Collegeville, Minnesota:
      The Liturgical press, August 11, 1974.
      Abortion and euthanasia discussed
      from a moral view with evils stated.
      Statistics cited.

86   Matthews, W. R.   "Voluntary euthanasia:
     the ethical aspect,"   EUTHANASIA AND THE
     RIGHT TO DEATH: THE CASE FOR VOLUNTARY
     EUTHANASIA. (Downing) London: Peter
     Owen, 1970. pp. 25-29.
       Though the endurance of pain and suffer-
     ing may produce grace, Matthews suggests
     that pain is evil. He recognizes that
     one can never be certain that any illness
     is incurable. He cannot, nevertheless,
     rationalize how anyone who has had any
     experience of visiting the sick can
     question the proposition that there are
     cases where nothing but useless agony
     can be anticipated.

87   Meier, Henk J.   MENSWAARDIG STERVEN
     EUTHANASIE IN DISCUSSIE. Hilversum:
     P. Brand, 1968.

88   Menezes, Evandro Correa de. DIREITO DE
     MATAR. Rio de Janiero: A. Noite, 194-.

89   Meyers, David W. "Euthanasia," THE HUMAN
     BODY AND THE LAW: A MEDICO-LEGAL STUDY.
     Edinburgh: University Press, 1970. pp.
     139-159.
       Treats euthanasia from the legal position
     as well as discusses its present status
     in Scotland, England, United States,
     Germany, Norway, Sweden, Switzerland and
     other countries.

90   Millard, C. K. EUTHANASIA: A PLEA FOR
     THE LEGALIZATION OF VOLUNTARY EUTHANASIA.
     Daniel, 1931.

91   Nettre, Georges. DISCOURS: L'EUTHANASIE.
     Besancon, Impr. de l' Est, 1954.

92   New York (State) Lib. Legis. Reference
     Section. EUTHANASIA: ARTICLES AND
     OPINIONS ON LEGALIZED MERCY KILLING.
     Compiled by June Lambert, December, 1946.
     Available through PAIS.

93   Niedermeyer, Albert.   HANBUCH DER SPEZIELLEN
      PASTORALMEDIZIN. Wein: Herder, 1949-52.

94   OUTLINES OF CRIMINAL LAW.   (Kenny) Turner,
      1952. pp. 14-51.
         Describes acts of omission where the
      patient is allowed to die as acts of
      criminal homicide.

95   "Parliament debates euthanasia 1936-1970,"
      YOUR DEATH WARRANT: THE IMPLICATIONS OF
      EUTHANASIA. (Gould) London: Chapman,
      1971, pp. 38-67.
         There have been four important debates
      on euthanasia in the United Kingdom Par-
      liament...of particular interest... as
      reflecting closely the arguments for and
      against euthanasia. The author describes
      previously rejected legislation and ends
      by discussing the changing argument--
      the 1969 debate.

96   Paul, Norman L. "Three neglected view-
      points," THE RIGHT TO DIE: DECISION AND
      DECISION MAKERS. New York: Jason Aronson,
      1974. p. 75.
         Selects views omitted in the discussion
      of euthanasia presented throughout the book.
      Considers the perspectives of the bereaved,
      the fear that the dying have been for-
      gotten and the right to die.

97   Paulus, Jacques. LE PROCES DE LA THALIDOMIDE.
      Paris: Gallimard, 1963. (French)

98   Pearson, Leonard. DEATH AND DYING: CURRENT
      ISSUES IN THE TREATMENT OF THE DYING
      PERSON. Case Western Reserve University
      Press, 1969.

99   Platen-Hallermund, Alice. DIE TOTUNG
      GEISTESKRANKER IN DEUTSCHLAND. Frank-
      furt om Main: Verlag der Frankfurter
      Hefte, 1948. (German)

100 PRINCIPLES OF CRIMINAL LAW. (Hall) 1947.
pp. 272-278.
Discusses omissions on the part of
the physician as a direct act, criminal
in nature, and thereby subject to criminal
prosecution.

101 QUESTIONS OF OUR DAY. "Movement for Euthanasia," by H. Ellis. New York: Vanguard
Press, 1936. pp. 302-304.

102 Rainey, J. EUTHANASIA OF DOGS AND CATS.
Balliere, 1933.

103 Ramsey, Paul. DEEDS AND RULES IN CHRISTIAN
ETHICS. New York: Scribner's, 1967.
Distinguishes between acts of omission
and acts of commission as related to
the practice of euthanasia.

104 Ramsey, Paul. THE PATIENT AS PERSON; EXPLOR-
ATIONS IN MEDICAL ETHICS. New Haven:
Yale University Press, 1970.
A book about ethics written by a
Christian ethicist. Topics discussed
include not confusing death with extraordinary means, contrasting ordinary
and extraordinary means and the morality
of caring for the dying patient.

105 Reiner, Silvain. ET LA TERRE SERA PURE.
Paris: Fayard, 1969.

106 Roberts, Harry. EUTHANASIA AND OTHER ASPECTS
OF LIFE AND DEATH. London: Constable
& Co. Ltd., 1936. Also published by:
Toronto: Macmillain, 1936.
The relationship between the doctor
and the patient is discussed in the light
of legal implications of voluntary euthan-
asia.

107 Rosenberg, Lotte. IS THE SANCTITY OF LIFE
ABSOLUTE? London: Essex and Suffolk
Quarterly Meeting of the Society of Friends,
1966.

108 Rostand, Jean. HUMANLY POSSIBLE. New
     York: Saturday Review Press, 1973.
     A French biologist asserts that human
     life should be prolonged no matter how
     useless it becomes.

109 Rubel, Robert. THE EUTHANASIA OF POLITICS:
     THE POLITICAL THOUGHT OF MAYNARD KEYS.
     University of Chicago, 1969. (Dissertation)

110 RUSTIC MORALIST. "Euthanasia," by W. R.
     Inge. New York: Putnam, 1937. pp. 194-
     198.

111 Safar, P. RESUSCITATION-CONTROVERSIAL
     ASPECTS. Berlin: Springer-Verlag, 1963.

112 St. John-Stevas, Norman. THE RIGHT TO
     New York: Holt, Rinehart and Winston,
     1964. Also published by: London:
     Hodder and Stoughton, 1963.
     Discusses the thalidomide tragedy, the
     beginning of life, a right to die, a
     right to kill oneself, the State's
     right to kill and the right to kill in
     times of war.

113 "A sample of medical attitudes," YOUR
     DEATH WARRANT: THE IMPLICATIONS OF EUTHAN-
     ASIA. (Gould) London: Chapman, 1971.
     pp. 117-124.
     Reports the opinions and attitudes of
     physicians and nurses replying to a
     questionnaire involving euthanasia and
     general care of the dying patient.

114 Sanchez Valer, Vincente. EL PROBLEMA
     MORAL-RELIGIOSO DE LA EUTANASIA.
     Lima, Peru, 1951.

115 Schlaich, Ludwig F. LEBENSUNWERT?KIRCHE
     UND INNERE MISSION WURTTEMBERGS IM KAMPF
     GEGEN DIE VERNICHTUNG LEBENSUNWERTEN LEBENS.
     Stuttgart: Quell-Verlag der Evang,
     Gesellschaft, 1947. (German)

116 Schmidt, Gerhard. SELEKTION IN DER HEIL-
      ANSTALT 1939-1945. Stuttgart: Evan-
      gelische Verlagswerk, 1965. (German)

117 Schoenberg, Bernard, et al. PSYCHOSOCIAL
      ASPECTS OF TERMINAL CARE--SYMPOSIUM.
      New York: Columbia University Press,
      1972.
         Examines sudden cardiac death, problems
      generated by a child's death, the behavior
      and attitude of the doctor of a terminally
      ill patient, pain control, geriatrics,
      bereavement,and institutional care.
      Specific treatment by euthanasia is
      considered. (14 bibliographical refs.)

118 Slater, Eliot. "Death: the biological
      aspect," EUTHANASIA AND THE RIGHT TO
      DEATH. (Downing) London: Peter Owen,
      1970. pp. 50-60.
         Examines principles on which primary
      issues of life and death are based and
      discusses the means some go to in order
      to prevent death.

119 Smith, Harmon L. ETHICS AND THE NEW
      MEDICINE. New York: Abingdon, 1970.
         In the section title : "Death and the
      Care of the Dying", the Christian ethic
      as it pertains to abortion and euthanasia
      is analyzed.(pp. 154-164)

120 Soares, Vincente. DIRECTO DE MATAR ANTE
      A MEDICINA. Instituto Bibliografico,
      Brasileiro, 1948.

121 Spencer, Herbert. "Speculation and euthan-
      asia," FACTS AND COMMENTS. Plainview,
      N. Y.: Books for Libraries, 1902, rep.
      1973. Also published by: New York:
      Appleton-Century-Crofts, 1933.

122 Steinbauer, Gustav. DIE EUTHANASIE IN
      LICHTE DES NURNBERGER ARZTEPROZESSES.
      Wien: Kapri, 1949. (German)

123 Stichting Landelijk Orgaan van de Gere-
     formeerde Gezindte voor de Bejaardenzory.
     EUTHANASIE EN DE BIJAARDE MENS. RAPPORT
     VAN EEN STUDIE ROND DE VERSCHILLENDE
     ASPECTEN VAN HET VRAAGSTUK DER EUTHANASIE
     EN DE VERLENGING VAN HET LEVEN, MET NAME
     GERICHT AP DE BIJAARD MENS. Utrecht,
     1968.

124 Strandberg, Brynjulf. BARMJERTIGHEDSRAB
     OG LARGEGERNIG. Gyldenal, 1965.

125 Study Group on Euthanasia. YOUR DEATH WARRANT
     THE IMPLICATIONS OF EUTHANASIA: A MEDICAL,
     LEGAL AND ETHICAL STUDY. London: Chapman,
     1971.
        This work consists of a series of essays
     treating medical, legal and ethical aspects
     of euthanasia. Each essay in the volume
     appears in this section of the bibliography
     with full annotations.

126 Sullivan, Joseph Vincent. CATHOLIC TEACHING
     ON THE MORALITY OF EUTHANASIA. Catholic
     University of America, 1949.

127 Sullivan, Joseph Vincent. MORALITY OF
     MERCY KILLING. Westmenster, Maryland:
     Newman Press, 1950.
        Discusses the Catholic theological
     teachings and beliefs with regard to
     mercy killing. Includes the text of the
     American Euthanasia Bill.

128 Thevenin, Jean. J'AI TUE MON ENFANT.
     Paris: Editions Publications Premiere,
     1970.

129 Thompson, F. Conyers. "Death--a review of
     psychiatric considerations," THE RIGHT TO
     DIE: DECISIONS AND DECISION MAKERS.
     New York: Jason Aronson, 1974. pp. 7-14.
        Reviews psychiatric aspect of dying as
     it relates to life prolonging measures,
     such as transplantation medicine, cost of
     hospital care. Emphasizes full human life.

130   Thompson, Prescott W. "The loneliness of
         dying and the wish to die," THE RIGHT
         TO DIE: DECISION AND DECISION MAKERS.
         New York: Jason Aronson, 1974. pp. 50-52.
            Describes briefly four experiences that
         epitomize what Thompson has learned about
         the central importance of loneliness in
         the anticipation of death, and about the
         validity and effectiveness of the wish
         to die.

131   Till-d'Aulnis de Bouriull, HAH van.
         MEDISCH-JURIDISCHE ASPECTEN VAN HET
         MENSELIJK LEVEN. Deventer: Kluwer,
         1970.

132   Torrey, E. Fuller (ed). ETHICAL ISSUES IN
         MEDICINE. Boston: Little, Brown, 1968.
            Considers elective death, direct
         voluntary and indirect voluntary and
         direct involuntary and indirect involun-
         tary aspects of euthanasia.

133   Toynbee, Arnold. MAN'S CONCERN WITH DEATH.
         London: Hodder and Stroughton, 1968.

134   Trowell, Hugh. THE UNFINISHED DEBATE ON
         EUTHANASIA. London: S. C. M. Press,
         1973.
            Discusses the idea of euthanasia in
         relation to British doctors and British
         law. Examines Euthanasia Societies and
         problems encountered by these societies.
         Also contains an indepth analysis of
         the 1969 Voluntary Euthanasia Bill.

135   Trobo, R. AN ACT OF MERCY: EUTHANASIA.
         TODAY. Freeport, N. Y.: Nash Pub. Corp.
         1973.

136   Ullman, Montague, "Social dynamics and the
         right to die," THE RIGHT TO DIE: DECISION
         AND DECISION MAKERS. New York: Jason
         Aronson, 1974. pp. 21-26.
            Examines the collusive role played by
         societies in producing people unable to pick

21

the manner in which they will make their
exit from this world. Ullman also reviews
the social dynamics which surface
specifically at life's termination.

137 Valenzuela Madrid, Javier. EL HOMICIDO
     PEADOSO. Mexico, 1953.

138 Varwyk, Dietrich. DIE TOTUNG AUF VERLANGEN
     UND DIE BETEILIGUNG AM SUBSTMORD IM
     SCHWEIZERISCHEN, DEUTSCHEN UND FRANZ-
     OSISCHEN STRAFRECHT; Vergleichende
     Darstellung, Dusseldorf, 1964. (German)

139 Veach, Robert. DEATH AND DYING. Chicago:
     Claretian Publications, 1974.
        Examines variousfears and attitudes
     toward death with emphasis on religious
     attitudes.

140 Vere, Duncan Wright. SHOULD CHRISTIANS
     SUPPORT VOLUNTARY EUTHANASIA? London:
     Christian Medical Fellowship, 1971.
        The work is a seven page pamphlet which
     contains information on euthanasia from
     a medico-ethical and religious viewpoint.

141 Vere, Duncan Wright. VOLUNTARY EUTHANASIA:
     IS THERE AN ALTERNATIVE? London: Chris-
     tian Medical Fellowship, 1971
        States the Protestant-Christian viewpoint
     concerning euthanasia.

142 Visscher, M. B. (ed) HUMANISTIC PERSPECTIVES
     IN MEDICAL ETHICS. Buffalo, New York:
     Prometheus Books, 1972. pp.39-71.
        Considers the individual's right to
     die.

143 Weatherhead, Leslie. THE CHRISTIAN AGNOSTIC.
     London: Hodder and Stoughton, 1965.
        Argues for the right to voluntary
     euthanasia and for the maintenance of
     the dignity, beauty and meaning of life
     through a dignified death.

22

144 Weinberg, Jack. "Introduction," THE RIGHT
TO DIE: DECISION AND DECISION MAKERS.
New York: Jason Aronson, 1974. pp. 3-6.
A symposium focusing on individual's
right to die and the physician's duty to
consider the quality as well as the duration
of an existence.

145 Weizsacker, Viktor. EUTHANASIE UND MEN-
SCHENVERSUCHE. Heidelbirg: L. Schneider,
1947.

146 Wertenbaker, Lael Tucker. DEATH OF A MAN.
Boston: Beacon Press, 1954. rep. 1974.

147 "What the 1969 bill could have meant in
practice," YOUR DEATH WARRANT: THE
IMPLICATIONS OF EUTHANASIA. (Gould)
London: Chapman, 1971. pp. 107-116.
Examines the principle clauses of the 1969
Voluntary Euthanasia Bill in relation to
the patients, doctors and nurses who
would have been involved had it become law.

148 Williams, Glanville. "Euthanasia legislation:
a rejoinder to the non-religious objections,"
EUTHANASIA AND THE RIGHT TO DEATH: THE
CASE FOR VOLUNTARY EUTHANASIA. (Downing)
London: Peter Owen, 1970. pp. 134-147.
Argues for the acceptance of voluntary
euthanasia on the grounds that it will aid
in preventing unnecessary pain, and that
individuals should have the freedom to
choose.

149 Williams, Glanville L. THE SANCTITY OF
LIFE AND THE CRIMINAL LAW. New York:
Knopf, 1957. Also Published: London:
Faber, 1957.
Makes a comparison of the legal im-
plications involved with suicide and
euthanasia. Discusses euthanasia in
religious, criminal and legal light.
Infanticide, birth control, and abortion
are other topics included.

150 Williams, Robert H. ed. TO LIVE AND TO
    DIE: WHEN, WHY AND HOW. New York:
    Springer-Verlag, 1973.
      Considers alternatives to the per-
    formance of euthanasia such as, contra-
    ception, abortion, and suicide. The
    ethical dilemma associated with eu-
    thanasia is discussed, and the propa-
    gation, modification, and termination
    of life is studied.

SUBJECT INDEX TO
PERIODICAL LITERATURE

ABORTION

151 "Abortion and euthanasia," by S. Crosbie.
     ROCKY MOUNTAIN MEDICAL JOURNAL. 66:
     41-46, November, 1969.

152 "Abortion and euthanasia," by R. D.
     Lamm and S. Davison. ROCKY MOUNTAIN
     MEDICAL JOURNAL. 68:40-42, February,
     1971.
         "The conflict between abortion, under
     the 1967 Colorado abortion statute, and
     euthanasia found to exist by Dr. Crosbie
     is in actuality a non-existent problem.
     Neither in law, medicine or popular
     opinion is the abortion of an unquickened
     or non-viable fetus recognized as the
     taking of a 'life' of a human being.
     Permitting the termination of a pregnancy
     by abortion in the early months of preg-
     nancy consequently, is not in conflict
     with the rejection of euthanasia." p. 42.

153 "Drug that left a trail of heartbreak:
     thalidomide," LIFE. 53:24-36, August
     10, 1962.
         A pictorial documentary of the trials
     and heartbreaks caused by the infant-
     deforming drug, thalidomide, is presented
     in a series of successive articles.
     Individual cases of deformed infants,
     Dr. Kelsey's fortitude in keeping the
     drug off the U. S. markets, and the shock
     of the William S. Merrill Company are a
     few of the subjects reported in this
     issue.

154 "Euthanasia and abortion," by G. Williams.
     COLORADO LAW REVIEW. 38:178, Winter,
     1969.

155 "How do nurses feel about abortion and
     euthanasia?" by N. K. Brown et al.
     AMERICAN JOURNAL OF NURSING. 71:1413-
     1416, July, 1971.

Through a survey it was determined
that a higher proportion of nurses
received requests for euthanasia. And
paradoxically those nurses who are
farthest removed from day-to-day close
patient care are most in favor of euthanasia policies. (15 references)

156 "Infanticide," by J. C. M. Matheson.
MEDICO-LEGAL AND CRIMINOLOGICAL
REVIEW. 9:135-152, July, 1941.
Reviews medical questions involving
infanticide; presents statistics (including abortion); and discusses the
histories of several cases.

157 "License to live," CHRISTIANITY TODAY.
18:22-23, July 26, 1974.
With the acceptance of legalized
abortion comes the warning--first forced
sterilization once each family has
reached the optimum of three children;
next acceptance of passive euthanasia;
then active euthanasia. This editorial
calls upon christians to voice their
opposition to such measures.

158 "Power to kill; homicide as euthanasia,"
by M. Evans. AMERICAN OPINION. 17:
39-41, passim, January, 1974.
Offers a reflection on the incon-
sistencies of the public's attitude
toward abortion and euthanasia. Evans
reviews the implications of governmental
implementation of euthanasia and draws
considerable argumentative references
from the Commandment: Thou Shall Not
Kill.

159 "Pregnancy interruption and euthanasia,"
by H. E. Ehrhardt. ARCHIV FUR KRIMIN-
OLOGIE. (Lubeck) 152:129-145, November
December, 1973. (German)

ABORTION

160 "Prolonging life - Part 3: The hope in
experiment," by J. Pells. NURSING
TIMES. 70:352-353, March 7, 1974.
"The dangers in experimental surgery,
abortion and euthanasia are discussed
by the author in the third of six articles.
These articles were originally submitted
as an essay for the Bailliere Tindall
Prize for Nursing studies in 1972." p. 352.

IN ANIMALS

161 "American Veterinary Medical Association
condones use of decompression chambers
as one of the most satisfactory methods
of animal euthanasia," NEW YORK TIMES.
(Newspaper). 41:5, March 2, 1972.

162 "CO_2 euthanasia in cats," by J. B. Glen,
et al. THE VETERINARY RECORD. 90:644,
May 27, 1972.
Preliminary information suggests that
CO_2 has advantages over chloroform as
an agent for euthanasia for cats because
loss of consciousness occurs faster
and no marked excitement has been noted
by Dr. J. B. Glen and W. N. Scott.

163 "Carbon dioxide euthanasia of cats," by
J. B. Glen and W. N. Scott. BRITISH
VETERINARY JOURNAL. 129(5):471-479,
1973. (In English with English, French,
German, and Spanish summaries).
Euthanasia of eleven adult cats and
twenty kittens was carried out in a U.
F.A.W. Euthanasia Cabinet, and the times
of loss of consciousness, respiratory
arrest and death noted. Cages were
primed with CO_2 gas of concentrations
varying from 28-79%. O_2 range concomitant
was 15-47. CO_2 provides a suitable
alternative to chloroform for euthanasia
of cats by non-veterinary personnel
employed by Animal Welfare societies.

164 "Effect of magnesium ions on neuromuscular
transmission in the horse, steer and
dog," by John M. Bowen, D. M. Blackman
and James E. Heavner. JOURNAL OF THE
AMERICAN VETERINARY MEDICAL ASSOCIATION.
157(2):164-173, 1970.
  "Infusion of magnesium sulfate at a
dosage of 0.22g/kg was lethal in one horse
due to respiratory paralysis and cardiac
arrest. Dosages recommended for euthanasia were adequate for production of
complete neuromuscular block and death
due to asphyxia." (BA) The authors
suggest that this method is inhumane and
should be abandoned.

165 "Equine euthanasia," by N. C. Roberts.
JOURNAL OF THE AMERICAN VETERINARY
MEDICAL ASSOCIATION. 129(7):328, October,
1956.
  The euthanizing of horses has proven
to be a difficult operation. This article
reports a method of injecting sodium N-
amylethylbarbiturate and sodium sec-
butylethylbarbiturate into the animals.

166 "Euthanasia in mink-a survey of methods
used in killing mink for removal of the
fur," by G. Loftsgard. NORDSK
VETERINAERTIDSSKRIFT (Norway). 82(9):
492-496, 1970.
  In Norwegian law, four ways of killing
domestic animals are permitted: blow
against the head; bolt in the forehead
or shot; electrical apparatus and phar-
macological anesthetics or poisons.
Each method is examined in detail.

167 "Euthanasia in s all animals," by J. F.
Ruff. MICHIGAN STATE COLLEGE
VETERINARIAN. 5(4):151, 173, 1945.
  Five to ten ml. of formalin is injected
intracardially with a 3-inch 18-gauge
needle; cardiac activity immediately stops.

168 "Euthanasia of equines. (The action of
     magnesium)," by J. R. Hodgkins, M.
     Ragheb, H. I. Abdou and M. Nashed.
     VETERINARY RECORD. 55(28):269-270, 1943.
        An 80% solution of $MgSO_4$ was injected
     intravenously from enema douche and
     a suitable needle. The optimum death
     time was reported as 2.5 minutes.

169 "Euthanasia property rights in bodies -
     necropsies," by H. W. Hannah. JOURNAL
     OF THE AMERICAN VETERINARY MEDICAL
     ASSOCIATION. 163:1352, passim, December
     15, 1973.
        States a veterinarian does not have
     the right to euthanize an animal without
     the consent of its owner. An analysis is
     presented with discussions of other modes
     of death for animals.

170 "Magnesium sulfate for euthanasia in dogs,"
     by J. B. Aranez and L. B. Caday. JOURNAL
     OF THE AMERICAN VETERINARY MEDICAL
     ASSOCIATION. 133(4):213, August 15, 1958.
        Magnesium sulfate is inexpensive and is
     widely available as a useful and humane
     drug for euthanizing dogs. A table of
     data on an experiment conducted on 48
     dogs that were injected with magnesium
     sulfate is included in the article.

171 "Mass euthanasia for dogs with carbon
     monoxide and/or carbon dioxide: pre-
     liminary trials," by A. H. Carding.
     JOURNAL OF SMALL ANIMAL PRACTICE.
     9(5):245-259, 1968. (French and German
     summaries).
        Recommends alternatives to the present
     methods of killing unwanted dogs.
     Describes a CO and CO_2 chamber used in
     Japan. Minimal hazards and risks are
     encountered. Lethal dosages are described
     as well as recommendations for this
     method's use for euthanasia.

172 "Morbital w eutanzji malych zwierzat,
    (Morbital in the euthanasia of small
    animals)," by R. Badura. MEDYCYNA
    WETERYNARYJNA. 28(8):481-482, 1972.
        Morbital series 14 is a mercy killing
    preparation used in the Warsaw Veterin-
    ary Institute (Poland) for euthanasia
    of small animals. 16% pentabarbital is
    administered I. V., I. C., or I. P.
    Death time reports are given. In case
    of need, the prepartion is given I. V.

173 "The question of euthanasia," by A. I.
    Stern. JOURNAL OF THE AMERICAN VETER-
    INARY MEDICAL ASSOCIATION. 118(888):
    150-151, March, 1951.
        The use of euthanasia in veterinary
    medicine should be deemphasized. In-
    stead, emphasis should be placed on the
    development of greater skill in animal
    surgery and care and in establishing
    better relationships with pet owners.

174 "Report of the AVMA Panel on Euthanasia,"
    JOURNAL OF THE AMERICAN VETERINARY MEDI-
    CAL ASSOCIATION. 142:162-170, January 15,
    1963.
        Analyzes many agents by which euthana-
    sia is employed on animals. Inhalants,
    noninhalant parenteral preparations, and
    mechanical devices are reviewed in terms
    of their advantages and/or disadvantages
    in veterinary practice.

175 "Report of the AVMA panel on euthanasia,"
    JOURNAL OF THE AMERICAN VETERINARY MEDI-
    CAL ASSOCIATION. 160:761-772, March 1,
    1972.
        Behavioral considerations and an eval-
    uation of methods of euthanasia is dis-
    cussed. The pros and cons of inhalant
    and noninhalant agents are reviewed. The
    physical methods of animal euthanasia such
    as electrocution, shooting, hypoxia in-

duced by rapid decompression and other methods, and a few other physical methods are examined. Beneath each discussion of a euthanasia method are the advantages and disadvantages, and recommendations.

176 "Respiratory artifact produced by CO_2 and pentabarbitone sodium euthanasia in rats," by J. K. Fawell, et al. LABORATORY ANIMALS (England). 6(3): 321-326, 1972. (German and French summaries)
   Perivascular edema was observed in the lungs of the rats that were killed by CO_2 euthanasia. An increased incidence of extravasation of blood was observed in these animals as compared to that seen in the lungs of rats killed by pentabarbitone sodium.

177 "Small animal euthanasia," by R. F. Gentry. VETERINARY MEDICINE. 40:248-249, July, 1945.
   Analyzes various methods which might be employed in small animal euthanasia. Precautions are discussed with each method.

178 "Small animal euthanasia chamber," by H. S. Rudolph. LABORATORY ANIMAL CARE. 13: 91-95, April, 1963.
   Presents a detailed description of the construction of a CO_2 euthanasia chamber with pictures and detailed diagrams.

CANCER

179 "A better way to die," by Donald Gould. NEW STATESMAN. 77:474-475, April, 1969.
   A comparison of the treatment of cancer patients at two institutions sheds light into the type of treatment that should be available to cancer patients and their families. A glowing report of the work being done by Dr. Cecily Saunders and staff at the St. Christopher's

Hospice in Syndenham for terminally ill patients is cited. A major tenant in this article is that legalized euthanasia is the easiest option to take because it is not difficult to persuade an unhappy person that he is better off dead; however, it is far more difficult to restore to the desperate person that life can still be worth living. p. 475.

180 "Cancer and conscience," TIME. 78:60, November 3, 1961.
Withholding aggressive or extraordinary treatment to far gone cancer patients and telling the patient the truth about his diagnosis were subjects of talks given at the annual meeting of the American Cancer Society in Manhattan.

181 "Care of the patient with advanced malignant disease," ARIZONA MEDICINE. 19:179-187, August, 1962.
A Catholic bishop, an Internist, an Orthopedist, a Radiologist, a Psychiatrist, an Oncologist and a Research Clinician express their views on cancer patient care.

182 "The development of emotional complications in the patient with cancer," by R. Senescu. JOURNAL OF CHRONIC DISEASES. 16:813, 1963.

183 "Doctor at the bar," NEWSWEEK. 35:20, January 16, 1950.
The trial of Dr. Hermann Sander has begun. Dr. Sander is accused of administering a fatal injection of air into his cancer-ridden patient, Abbie Borroto's vein.

184 "L'euthanasie," by H. Bouquet. REVUE GENERALE DES SCIENCES PURE ET APPLIQUES. 44:532-534, October 15, 1933. (French)

Bouquet discusses euthanasia as it relates to the terminally ill cancer patient. He considers the administration of drugs to the dying patient to make the event of death less painful.

185 "Euthanasia," by H. Roberts. NEW STATESMAN AND NATION. 10:630-631, November 2, 1935.
States that those forms of active euthanasia used to relieve the pain and suffering of the terminally ill cancer patient are gaining in support among medical personnel.

186 "Euthanasia and pain in cancer," by A. Ravich. ACTA; UNIO INTERNATIONALES CONTRA CANCRUM. (Louvain) 9(2):397-399, 1953.
One of the most difficult situations one must face is the dying cancer patient who is in tremendous pain. In such situations euthanasia gains accept-ability. Ravich discusses the social mores which construct a barrier to the acceptance of euthanasia socially. Moreover, he stresses the fact that some cancer pain can now be controlled.

187 "Father killer," NEWSWEEK. 35:21, February 13, 1950.
Carol Paight's father was found to have cancer. As an act of mercy, Miss Paight fatally wounded her father.

188 "For love or pity," TIME. 55:15-16, February 6, 1950.
The story of Carol Paight, who shot her cancer-ridden father in an act of mercy killing, is reported.

189 "Forty cc of air," TIME. 55:13-14, January 9, 1950.
Time reporters relate the circumstances

causing the death of Mrs. Abbie Borroto.
Insinuation is made that she died as a
result of active euthanasia performed by
her physician, Dr. Hermann Sander.

190 "If that can be murder," NEWSWEEK. 35:
41, January 30, 1950.
Dr. Abraham Lincoln Goldwater discusses
the opportunities which he has had to
practice various forms of euthanasia
during his 78 years of life. References
are made to the Paight and Sander cases.

191 "Law of God," TIME. 55:20, January 16,
1950.
Dr. Hermann Sander injected forty cc
of air into the veins of a terminally ill
cancer patient as an act of mercy. TIME
reporters discuss the national attention
brought to the subject of euthanasia
through the publicity involved with the
case.

192 "May doctors kill?" by Harry Roberts.
LIVING AGE. 347:159-162, 1934.
Dr. Harry Roberts gives his answer to
the question, "May doctors kill?" When
sympathy outweighs the fear of the law,
act upon it. This principle is applicable
to cases where Dr. Roberts admits that he
would not hesitate to painlessly end the
life of a patient suffering from such a
painful disorder as cancer of the larynx;
however, he would also not be an enthusiast
for euthanasia unless such acts were
heavily safeguarded.

193 "Mercy killing debated: Chicago Wesley
Memorial Hospital," AMA NEWS. 10:9,
August 28, 1967.
Robert Waskin watched his mother suffer
through five hospital stays. Because
she was in pain, and because his entire
family was suffering mental agony and

acknowledging that his mother wished for death, he shot and killed her.

194 "Old lady slept," NEWSWEEK. 53:44, May 18, 1959.
An 80 year-old woman, dying with cancer, slept (with the aid of her physician) until she died. Newsweek reporters discuss the resultant controversy and public reaction to the woman's physician's actions.

195 "Problems of length of terminal care and disthanasia in patients with female genital cancer," by E. Klauber. CSEKOSLOVENSKA GYNEKOLOGIE. (Praha) 37: 176-179, April, 1972. (Sto.)

196 "Psychological aspects of cancer," by J. S. Stehlin and K. H. Beach. JOURNAL OF THE AMERICAN MEDICAL ASSOCIATION. 197 (2):140, July 11, 1966.

197 "Psychological reaction of the physician in cancer and euthanasia," by J. Schavelzon. ANAIS PAULISTAS DE MEDICINA E CIRURGIA. (Sao Paulo) 76(3):183-185, September, 1958.

198 "The right to die with dignity," by Stewart Alsop. GOOD HOUSEKEEPING. 179: 69, 130-132, August, 1974.
From his own experience, a distinguished journalist gives his personal viewpoint on the agonizing problems of euthanasia. He believes that a terminal patient should have the right to decide his fate and be able to receive sufficient doses of painkillers, including herion, to relieve suffering.

199 "Similar to murder," TIME. 55:20, March 6, 1950.

Dr. Hermann Sander injected 10cc of air four times into a vein of Mrs. Abbie Borroto, a terminally ill cancer patient in great pain. Mr. Borroto begged Dr. Sander to do something to eliminate his wife's pain, even if it was necessary to eliminate her life. As a direct result of a medical librarian's report, Dr. Sander stood prosecution for his actions.

200 "Unfinished debate," COMMONWEAL. 51: 619-621, March 24, 1950.
This article begins with an analysis of the much-publicized case of Dr. Hermann Sander. From this dialogue, the editorialist launches into a discussion of the Catholic role in the euthanasia question and expresses an opinion as to the Catholic's role in euthanasia conflicts.

201 "Vein injection case," NEWSWEEK. 35:19, January 9, 1950.
Reports the events surrounding the Sander case involving Dr. Hermann Sander's allegedly administering air into the veins of Mrs A. Borroto, his terminally ill cancer patient.

202 "Why prolong the life of a patient with advanced cancer?" by D. A. Karnofsky. CA: CANCER JOURNAL FOR CLINICIANS. (New York) 10:9-11, January-February, 1960.

SEE ALSO:
CASES OF MERCY KILLINGS

CASES OF MERCY KILLINGS

AUZELLO: NEWSPAPER ARTICLE

203 "C. Auzello kills wife who had incurable
     illness, then kills self," NEW YORK
     TIMES. 9:3, May 31, 1969.

BECKER

204 "The right to kill - continued," TIME.
     26:39-40, November 25, 1935.
        Miss Anna Becker, 34, was badly injured
     in an automobile crash. Her body has
     never been able to fully recover. She
     is constantly in pain. In a letter she
     wrote to a physician, she made a plea
     for her life to be ended. Legal opinions
     and an analysis of the "American psy-
     chology" are also included within the
     article.

BERMAN: NEWSPAPER ARTICLE

205 "Dr. A. J. Berman gets suspended sentence
     for '50 mercy killing of tubercular
     brother," NEW YORK TIMES. 11:3, March
     13, 1952.

BLACKFORD: NEWSPAPER ARTICLE

206 "Stabbing of W. M. Blackford by wife who
     attempts suicide called mercy killing,"
     NEW YORK TIMES. 26:6, June 2, 1948.

BRAUNSDORFF

207 "Murder or mercy," TIME. 55:20-21, June
     5, 1950.
        Eugene Braunsdorff shot his retarded
     daughter as an act of mercy. The court
     judged the case differently.

     NEWSPAPER ARTICLES

208 "E. Braunsdorff held in killing of spastic

daughter," NEW YORK TIMES. 28:8, June
25, 1949.

209 "E. Braunsdorff acquitted on insanity
grounds for killing daughter, Detroit,"
NEW YORK TIMES. 25:4, May 23, 1950.

BROWNHILL: NEWSPAPER ARTICLES

210 "Mrs. May Brownhill takes life of thirty-
one-year old, imbecile son," THE TIMES.
(London) 11:2, October 2, 1934.
Mrs. May Brownhill took her son's life
by giving him nearly one hundred aspirin
tablets and then placing a gas tube in
his mouth. She was facing a serious
operation and was concerned about the
fate of her son should she die.

211 "Sentenced to die for mercy killing of
imbecile son, Leeds," NEW YORK TIMES.
25:1, December 2, 1934.

212 "Mrs. Brownhill freed in mercy killing of
son, Leeds," NEW YORK TIMES. 3:2,
March 3, 1935.

BUTTS

213 "Deed of friendship: Mary Happer shot
by friend," NEWSWEEK. 65:30, April
26, 1965.
Dorothy Butts witnessed the constant
pain of her friend, Mary Happer. Miss
Butts ended Miss Happer's suffering
and then took her own life.

214 "Today I killed my best friend; Dorothy
Butts kills Mary Happer," TIME. 85:
74 passim, April 23, 1965.

CASES OF MERCY KILLINGS

CAHILL: NEWSPAPER ARTICLE

215   "D. W. Cahill kills wife, attempts suicide,
        Watertown," NEW YORK TIMES. 24:5,
        April 21, 1942.

CANNON: NEWSPAPER ARTICLES

216   "Mrs. T. Cannon held for slaying husband
        she says had cancer," NEW YORK TIMES.
        47:5, February 23, 1954.

217   "Cannon is indicted for murder," NEW YORK
        TIMES. 13:1, March 2, 1954.

218   "Cannon held insane," NEW YORK TIMES.
        13:1, March 26, 1954.

COLLINS: NEWSPAPER ARTICLES

219   "F. M. Collins kills son who is mental
        patient," NEW YORK TIMES. 8:4, May 5,
        1952.

220   "Collins arraigned for murder," NEW YORK
        TIMES. 40:1, May 6, 1952.

COWAN: NEWSPAPER ARTICLE

221   "M. L. Cowan kills sister, Mrs. L. Saeger,"
        NEW YORK TIMES. 17:2, August 16, 1939.

DUEBEN, BARONESS von: NEWSPAPER ARTICLES

222   "Sentenced to three months on charge of
        assisting mother, Baroness von Dueben,
        to commit suicide," NEW YORK TIMES.
        9:1, May 24, 1932.

223   "Pardoned by King Christian for 'mercy
        slaying' of mother, Baroness von Dueben,"

CASES OF MERCY KILLINGS

> NEW YORK TIMES. 8:2, July 2, 1932.

ELDRIDGE: NEWSPAPER ARTICLE

224 "A. S. Eldridge freed after coroner's
     jury ordered trial for role in ill
     sister's suicide," NEW YORK TIMES.
     44:5, November 29, 1958.

FINKLIENE: NEWSPAPER ARTICLE

225 "Mrs Finkliene sees Sweedish doctor, two
     deformed babies born; mother held, Liege,
     for killing deformed baby," NEW YORK
     TIMES. 19:1, August 8, 1962.

FRENCH: NEWSPAPER ARTICLES

226 "Dr. Towneley Thorndike French kills wife,"
     NEW YORK TIMES. 8:5, September 7, 1932.

227 "Dr. French sentenced to fifteen to twenty
     years for killing wife," NEW YORK TIMES.
     4:4, December 3, 1932.

GILPATRIC: NEWSPAPER ARTICLE

228 "J. G. Gilpatric kills wife and self after
     discovery that she has cancer," NEW
     YORK TIMES. 28:8, July 8, 1950 and also
     related information found: 52:5, July
     9, 1950.

GRAY: NEWSPAPER ARTICLE

229 "A. Gray put on probation in killing of
     son, apparently incurably ill," NEW
     YORK TIMES. 1:4, October 7, 1965.

GREENFIELD

230 "Better off dead: Greenfield case," TIME.
     33:24, January 23, 1939.

CASES OF MERCY KILLINGS

Louis Greenfield chloroformed his 17-year old imbecile son. The controversy surrounding the case and general attitudes toward euthanasia are reviewed.

231 "Taking life legally," MAGAZINE DIGEST, 1947.
Presents Louis Greenfield's testimony concerning his actions in the mercy killing of his 17-year old imbecile son. Greenfield claims that his actions were against the law of man but not against the law of God. He was acquitted.

NEWSPAPER ARTICLES

232 "Louis Greenfield held for homicide after chloroforming son, Jerome, because the boy was incurable," NEW YORK TIMES. 3:1, January 13, 1939.

233 "Louis Greenfield arraigned; permitted to attend funeral," NEW YORK TIMES. 32:6, January 14, 1939.

234 "Louis Greenfield indicted," NEW YORK TIMES. 2:5, January 18, 1939.

235 "Greenfield pleads not guilty; released on bail," NEW YORK TIMES. 9:4, January 19, 1939.

236 "Louis Greenfield to go on trial for death of son, Jerome," NEW YORK TIMES. 36:4, April 29, 1939.

237 "Louis Greenfield on trial for death of imbecile son, Jerome," NEW YORK TIMES. 48:1, May 9, 1939.

238 "Dr. I. N. Kugelmass testifies son was a menace," NEW YORK TIMES. 6:5, May 10, 1939.

CASES OF MERCY KILLINGS

239 "Greenfield says he slew at God's
       command," NEW YORK TIMES. 10:2, May
       11, 1939.

240 "Greenfield acquitted," NEW YORK TIMES.
       May 12, 1939.

HAUNG: NEWSPAPER ARTICLE

241 "Mrs. E. Haung admits killing invalid
       mother, Ms. K. Latshaw, Reading, Pa.,"
       NEW YORK TIMES. June 23, 1947.

HEFELMANN: NEWSPAPER ARTICLES

242 "Hefelmann trial opens...reportedly sought
       mercy death for his own mother," NEW
       YORK TIMES. 5:2, February 19, 1964.

243 "Hefelmann trial," NEW YORK TIMES. 2:5,
       February 20, 1964.

244 "Hefelmann testifies," NEWYORK TIMES.
       5:1, February 25, 1964.

245 "Hefelmann details program to kill mentally
       and physically retarded; says doctors
       were volunteers dedicated to the idea
       of mercy deaths," NEW YORK TIMES. 13:1,
       February 26, 1964.

246 "Hefelmann details program says Drs. Catel,
       Wentzler and Hinze made life-or-death
       rulings," NEW YORK TIMES. 11:1, Feb-
       ruary 27, 1964.

247 "Hefelmann charges Roman Catholic Church
       was willing to tolerate mass 'mercy'
       killings," NEW YORK TIMES. 9:4, April
       8, 1964.

248 "Hefelmann trial, recessed because of his
       health, to resume," NEW YORK TIMES.
       3:1, July 26, 1964.

CASES OF MERCY KILLINGS

249 "Hefelman trial postponed indefinitely,"
     NEW YORK TIMES. 5:6, August 29, 1964.

HENRY: NEWSPAPER ARTICLE

250 "R. Henry held for killing 8-year-old
     son crippled by polio, Rochelle, Illinois,"
     NEW YORK TIMES. 47:7, November 2, 1950.

HEYDE: NEWSPAPER ARTICLE

251 "Hesse state to try Drs. W. Heyde, G. Bohne
     and H. Hefelmann for mercy killings,"
     NEW YORK TIMES. 2:4, July 24, 1962.

     SEE ALSO:
       HEFELMANN: NEWSPAPER ARTICLES

HEYE: NEWSPAPER ARTICLE

252 "R. Heye kills invalid son, San Antonio,
     commits suicide," NEW YORK TIMES. 20:9,
     February 8, 1948.

INGALLS: NEWSPAPER ARTICLE

253 "Professor J. W. Ingalls dies in attempt
     to kill mentally ill and crippled
     daughter, Florence; two found in improvised
     gas chamber; daughter critically ill,"
     NEW YORK TIMES. 36:1, July 25, 1947.

JOHNSON, GEORGE E.

254 "Quality of mercy; mongoloid son," TIME.
     76:64, July 11, 1960
        George E. Johnson took the life of
     his thalidomide-deformed son.

JOHNSON, H. C.: NEWSPAPER ARTICLES

255 "H. C. Johnson held for murder in killing
     by gas of wife, Jennie, cancer victim,"
     NEW YORK TIMES. 1:3, October 2, 1938.

CASES OF MERCY KILLINGS

256 "Johnson found temporarily insane," NEW
    YORK TIMES. 30:4, October 12, 1938.
    Also related information may be found
    Section IV, 9:7, October 16, 1938.

257 "Johnson freed," NEW YORK TIMES, 46:1,
    October 19, 1938.

JONES

258 "Compassion," TIME. 62:11-12, July 27,
    1953.
        A report of a case involving the
    electrocution of a crippled diabetic
    wife by her husband, William R. Jones
    is briefly discussed.

KILBORN: NEWSPAPER ARTICLE

259 "R. Kilborn freed in mercy killing of
    wife who wounded self in suicide attempt,
    Cabourg, Ontario," NEW YORK TIMES.
    12:6, March 23, 1950.

KLAFT-SALUS: NEWSPAPER ARTICLE

260 "Incurable cripple killed by Dr. P. Klaft-
    Salus with consent of mother; she and
    mother arrested on murder charge: both
    released on mental irresponsibility
    pleas, and committed to asylum," NEW
    YORK TIMES. IV. 3:4, December 11,
    1932.

LONG

261 "Goodbye; how G. R. Long killed his
    daughter," TIME. 48:32, December 2,
    1946.
        G. R. Long put to a merciful death
    his seven-year-old deformed, imbecile
    daughter. The act and events surrounding
    the mercy killing are discussed.

CASES OF MERCY KILLINGS

262   "G. R. Long pleads guilty to killing
      daughter; sentenced. NYC Protestant
      Clergymen," NEW YORK TIMES. 25:2,
      October 10, 1946.

263   "Gordon Long gassed his deformed and
      imbecile seven-year-old daughter to death,"
      THE TIMES. (London). 2:7, November 23,
      1946.

264   "Long euthanasia case," THE TIMES.
      (London) 2:7, November 29, 1946.

LONGEVIN: NEWSPAPER ARTICLE

265   "Mrs. Longevin charged with murder for
      slaying epileptic son," NEW YORK TIMES.
      26:6, November 2, 1955.

MARPLES: NEWSPAPER ARTICLE

266   "J. S. Marples, who was jailed for slaying
      ill mother, hailed on return home," NEW
      YORK TIMES. 16:5, June 10, 1959.

MOHR: NEWSPAPER ARTICLES

267   "H. Mohr held in alleged mercy killing
      of brother," NEW YORK TIMES. 45:5,
      March 12, 1950.

268   "H. Mohr indicted in mercy killing of
      brother--Allentown, Pa.," NEW YORK TIMES.
      60:4, April 4, 1950.

269   "Mohr gets three years," NEW YORK TIMES.
      20:5, April 11, 1950.

270   "H. Mohr convicted of voluntary man-
      slaughter," NEW YORK TIMES. 26:1, April
      28, 1950.

CASES OF MERCY KILLINGS

MONTEMARANO

271 "Pathologists clash at Montemarano trial,"
    MEDICAL WORLD NEWS. 15:15, February 22,
    1974.
        Dr. Vincent A. Montemarano stood accused
    in the mercy killing of Eugene Bauer by
    injecting 5cc of potassium into his veins.
    The testimony of the trial as well as the
    innocent verdict is reported.

NEWSPAPER ARTICLES

272 "Lester Zygmaniak and Dr. Vincent A.
    Montemarano are both charged with committing
    euthanasia," THE NATIONAL OBSERVER.
    7/7-6, 1973.

273 "Dr. Vinvent A. Montemarano, former chief
    resident at Nassau County Medical Center
    (NY), is scheduled for trial on January
    14 on murder stemming from so-called mercy
    killing of cancer patient, Eugene Bauer,"
    NEW YORK TIMES. 44:4, January 13, 1974.

274 "Bauer, Eugenc (? - 1972): four men and
    four women jurors selected in trial of Dr.
    Vincent A. Montemarano ... who has been
    charged in death of dying cancer patient,"
    NEW YORK TIMES. 43:7, January 16, 1974.
    Also: "Two more jurors chosen," NEW YORK
    TIMES. 43:6, January 17, 1974.

275 "District Attorney William Cahn and his
    role as prosecutor in trial of Dr.
    Vincent A. Montemarano," NEW YORK TIMES.
    35:1, January 22, 1974.

276 "Nassau County, District Attorney, says he
    will prove that alleged slaying of
    terminally ill cancer patient Eugene
    Bauer by Dr. Montemarano was ... murder
    of convenience," NEW YORK TIMES. 35:4,
    January 22, 1974.

CASES OF MERCY KILLINGS

277 "Nurse Clara Miles testifies she saw Montemarano inject fatal dose," NEW YORK TIMES
34:4, January 24, 1974.

278 "Nassau County Detective William J. Lucas
quotes Dr. Vincent A. Montemarano...
"I did something unethical," NEW YORK
TIMES 65:5, January 25, 1974.

279 "Nassau County Medical Center surgery
department chairman Dr. Anthony DiBene-
detto testifies that Dr. Montemarano
confessed killing a terminally ill cancer patient," NEW YORK TIMES. 1:1,
January 26, 1974.

280 "Mrs. Rose Bauer testified that Dr. Montemarano requested permission for autopsy;
Nassau County Medical Examiner says
death was caused by injection of potassium
chloride," NEW YORK TIMES. 73:2, January
27, 1974.

281 "Reviews of testimony at trial of Dr. Vincent A. Montemarano," NEW YORK TIMES.
IV. p. 5, January 27, 1974.

282 "Nassau County Medical Center surgery department chairman testifies that Bauer could
have been dead before injection," NEW
YORK TIMES. 66:1, January 29, 1974.

283 "Nassau County Medical Examiner testifies
that Eugene Bauer died as a result of
potassium injection," NEW YORK TIMES.
70:3, January 30, 1974.

284 "Nassau County deputy chief medical examiner
Dr. Minoru Araki testifying at trial of
Dr. Vincent A. Montemarano attributes the
death of Eugene Bauer to injection of
potassium chloride," NEW YORK TIMES. 65:
6, January 31, 1974.

CASES OF MERCY KILLINGS

285   "Dr. Alfred Angrist testifies that death of Eugene Bauer was due to cancer and pulmonary embolism, not injection administered by Dr. Vincent A. Montemarano," NEW YORK TIMES. 26:6, February 1, 1974.

286   "Eight witnesses for defense testify that Dr. Vincent A. Montemarano is competent, dedicated and truthful," NEW YORK TIMES. 30:2, February 2, 1974.

287   "Lawrence K. Altman analyses of Eugene Bauer's death discusses problems of doctor's relationship with dying patient... meaning of euthanasia," NEW YORK TIMES. 15:1, February 4, 1974.

288   "Dr. Vincent A. Montemarano is found not guilty," NEW YORK TIMES. 1:1, February 6, 1974.

289   "Review of key moments in Vincent A. Montemarano trial, who was found innocent in death of cancer patient, Eugene Bauer," NEW YORK TIMES. 98:3, February 10, 1974.

290   "Review of Montemarano decision," NEW YORK TIMES. IV. p. 6, February 10, 1974.

291   "Dr. Vincent A. Montemarano, who was acquitted in February of charge that he had killed terminally ill cancer patient who was expected to die within 48 hours, is currently practicing in Rice Lake, Wisconsin," NEW YORK TIMES. 27:1, August 18, 1974.

NAGLE: NEWSPAPER ARTICLES

292   "H. H. Nagle slays invalid daughter," NEW YORK TIMES. 31:1, September 7, 1953.

293   "Nagle acquitted," NEW YORK TIMES. 20:7, December 24, 1953.

CASES OF MERCY KILLINGS

NOXON: NEWSPAPER ARTICLES

294 "State Corrections Commissioner seeks pardon for J. F. Noxon for '44 murder," NEW YORK TIMES. 10:5, October 16, 1947.

295 "Governor Bradford reportedly asks pardon... for recommendation on J. F. Noxon pardon plea," NEW YORK TIMES. 66:6, December 15, 1948.

296 "Governor Bradford admits error in saying J. F. Noxon had chance to plead guilty to manslaughter; Noxon release seen," NEW YORK TIMES. 28:6, December 25, 1948.

297 "Immediate Noxon parole probable," NEW YORK TIMES. 13:5, December 30, 1948.

298 "Hearing set on J. F. Noxon, Jr. parole plea, Boston," NEW YORK TIMES. 16:3, January 4, 1949.

299 "Noxon permitted to leave Massachusetts," NEW YORK TIMES. 30:7, January 15, 1949.

300 "Governor denies mercy killing a factor in J. F. Noxon case death sentence commutation. NEW YORK TIMES. August 8, 42:4, 1949.

PAIGHT

301 "Father killer," NEWSWEEK. 35:21, February 13, 1950.
   Carol Paight's father was found to have cancer. Carol Paight, in an act to mercy killing, fatally shot her father.

302 "For love or pity," TIME. 55:15-16, February 6, 1950.
   The story of Carol Paight, who shot her cancer-ridden father-- an act of mercy killing, is reported.

CASES OF MERCY KILLINGS

PAIGHT: NEWSPAPER ARTICLES

303   "Daughter questioned in shooting of police
        Sgt. C. Paight, cancer victim,:   NEW YORK
        TIMES. 1:2, September 24, 1949.

304   "Murder charged," NEW YORK TIMES.   78:3,
        September 25, 1949.

305   Stamford Mayor G. T. Barrett and others urge
        leniency," NEW YORK TIMES. 40:3, Septem-
        ber 26, 1949.

306   "Funeral--C. Paight," NEW YORK TIMES.   18:
        1, September 27, 1949.

307   "C. Paight awaits grand jury action,"   NEW
        YORK TIMES. 53:1, October 2, 1949.

308   "C. Paight inquest," NEW YORK TIMES.   60:
        5, October 12, 1949.

309   "Girl held criminally liable," NEW YORK
        TIMES. 34:1, October 14, 1949.

310   "Trial of Miss Carol Paight for killing
        father, incurable cancer victim, to
        start in Bridgeport, Connecticutt," NEW
        YORK TIMES. 23:4, January 24, 1950.

311   "Girl to plead insanity, four jurors picked,"
        NEW YORK TIMES. 50:2, January 26, 1950.

312   "Paight testimony," NEW YORK TIMES.   3:1,
        January 27, 1950.

313   "Doctor testifies that girl was not sane
        when she shot father," NEW YORK TIMES.
        30:1, January 28, 1950.

314   "Mother testifies in trial of Miss Carol
        Paight for killing father," NEW YORK
        TIMES. 54:3, February 1, 1950.

CASES OF MERCY KILLINGS

315 "Psychiatrist says Miss Paight was insane at the time of shooting," NEW YORK TIMES. February 2, 1950.

316 "Miss Paight testifies," NEW YORK TIMES. 11:1, February 3, 1950.

317 "Paight testimony ends," NEW YORK TIMES. 28:1, February 4, 1950.

318 "Miss Paight acquitted on legal insanity grounds," NEW YORK TIMES. 1:2, February 8, 1950.

319 "Past cases noted, acquittals not uncommon," NEW YORK TIMES. 24:3, February 8, 1950.

320 "Miss Paight to return to college," NEW YORK TIMES. 54:3, April 2, 1950.

PASTMA

321 "Implications of mercy; case in the Netherlands," TIME. 101:70, March 5, 1973. An injection of 200 mg of morphine IV into the veins of Gertruida Pastma's mother by Dr. Pastma resulted in her death.

PERA: NEWSPAPER ARTICLE

322 "Incurably ill shot and killed by Father J. Pera, who kills self, San Francisco," NEW YORK TIMES. 3:8, January 26, 1934.

PETYO: NEWSPAPER ARTICLE

323 "J. Petyo held for slaying invalid wife," NEW YORK TIMES. 12:2, October 26, 1953.

PICQUEREAU: NEWSPAPER ARTICLE

324 "J. Picquereau acquitted, Liege, of murdering his wife to relieve her of her suffering; details," NEW YORK TIMES.

CASES OF MERCY KILLINGS

8:1, January 16, 1972.

PRICE: NEWSPAPER ARTICLE

325 "London court acquits J. Price in mercy
     killing of 6-year-old son," NEW YORK TIMES.
     47:7, December 26, 1971.

REICHERT: NEWSPAPER ARTICLES

326 "Mrs. J. Reichert held for murder of brother,"
     NEW YORK TIMES. 1:5, December 4, 1941.

327 "State rests case against Mrs. Reichert
     for brother's slaying," NEW YORK TIMES.
     15:5, June 27, 1942.

328 "Mrs. Reichert acquitted in Horne slaying,"
     NEW YORK TIMES. 23:5, July 2, 1942.

329 "Court commits Mrs. Reichert for observation,"
     NEW YORK TIMES. 19:4, July 3, 1942.

REPOUILLE: NEWSPAPER ARTICLES

330 "L. Repouille murders imbecile son, R. O.,"
     NEW YORK TIMES. 25:7, October 13, 1939.

331 "Repouille freed on bail," NEW YORK TIMES.
     20:2, October 16, 1939.

332 "L. Repouille pleads not guilty to murder
     of imbecile son," NEW YORK TIMES. 16:7,
     May 8, 1940.

333 "L. Repouille pleads guilty to murder of
     imbecile son, NYC," NEW YORK TIMES. 23:7,
     June 6, 1941.

334 "Repouille trial," NEW YORK TIMES. 34:2,
     December 6, 1941.

335 "Found guilty," NEW YORK TIMES. 27:7,
     December 10, 1941.

52

CASES OF MERCY KILLINGS

336 "Gets suspended sentence," NEW YORK TIMES. 44:1, December 25, 1941.

337 "U. S. Circuit Appeals Court rules L. Repouille's '39 slaying of imbecile son shows lack of 'good moral character,' denies naturalization petition," NEW YORK TIMES. 17:4, December 6, 1947.

SALLIN

338 "Doctor cleared in euthanasia case: Sweden," MEDICAL WORLD NEWS. 6:49, April 2, 1965.
Dr. Sallin discontinued I-V. nourishment in a dying 81-year-old female patient. The court concurred with the opinion of the Swedish National Board of Health that it was perfectly responsible and legitimate for a physician not to prolong life in a dying patient.

SANDER

339 "Forty cc of air," TIME. 55:13-14, January 9, 1950.
TIME reporters relate the circumstances causing the death of Mrs. Abbie Borroto. Insinuation is made that she died as a direct result of active euthanasia performed by her physician, Dr. Hermann Sander.

340 "Doctor at the bar," NEWSWEEK. 35:20, January 16, 1950.
The trial of Dr. Hermann Sander has begun. Dr. Sander stands accused of administering a fatal injection of air into the veins of a cancer-ridden patient, Mrs. Abbie Borroto.

341 "Law of God," TIME. 55:20, January 16, 1950.
Dr. Hermann Sander injected air into the veins of a cancer-ridden patient as an act of mercy and in order to relieve her

suffering. This very popular euthanasia case called national attention to the subject.

342   "Life and death; letters to the NEW YORK
       TIMES," TIME. 55:50, March 13, 1950.
       The case of Dr. Hermann Sander, involving
an alleged active euthanasia attempt
upon the life of a terminal cancer patient,
is used as a focal point around which
society's attitudes toward euthanasia are
discussed.

343   "Mercy killing," NEW REPUBLIC. 127:6,
       January, 1950.
       Dr. Hermann Sander proportedly injected
air into the veins of a terminally ill
cancer patient as an act of mercy. By
making special references to this case, the
author discusses support for acts of mercy
performed as assisted suicides.

344   "Similar to murder," TIME. 55:20, March 6,
       1950.
       Dr. Hermann Sander injected 10cc of air
four times into a vein of Mrs. Abbie Borroto,
a terminal cancer patient in great pain.
Mr. Borroto begged Dr. Sander to do something to eliminate his wife's pain even if
it became necessary to eliminate her life.
As a direct result of a Medical Records
Librarian's report, Dr. Sander was prosecuted because of the action he took.

NEWSPAPER ARTICLES

345   "Dr. H. N. Sander free on bail in mercy death
       of cancer patient, returns to practice,"
       NEW YORK TIMES. 15:2, January 1, 1950.

346   "90% of Canadia and Goffstown, N. H.
       residents sign petition backing Sander,"
       NEW YORK TIMES. 25:2, January 2, 1950.

CASES OF MERCY KILLINGS

347 "Sander indicted; 300 prominent Britons ask U. N. to declare mercy killing legal right," NEW YORK TIMES. 12:3, January 4, 1950.

348 "Sander faces loss of medical license," NEW YORK TIMES. 2:3, January 5, 1950.

349 "Sander pleads not guilty in court," NEW YORK TIMES. 23:5, January 6, 1950.

350 "Other cases reviewed," NEW YORK TIMES. IV. 2:5, January 8, 1950.

351 "Trial of Sander set for February 20," NEW YORK TIMES. 54:1, January 12, 1950.

352 "Unitarian ministers back Sander," NEW YORK TIMES. 19:3, January 25, 1950.

353 "Trial of Dr. Hermann Sander in death of cancer patient to begin; case reviewed," NEW YORK TIMES. 12:3, February 19, 1950.

354 "Congregation of Candia Congregational Church prays for acquittal," NEW YORK TIMES. 42:3, February 20, 1950.

355 "Nine men chosen for jury; Catholic issue emerges during questioning of prospective juror," NEW YORK TIMES. 1:6, February 21, 1950.

356 "State will not ask death penalty; more jurors chosen," NEW YORK TIMES. 50:1, February 22, 1950.

357 "Jury visits scene of death; questions put to jurors before selection cited," NEW YORK TIMES. 23:1, February 23, 1950.

358 "Wife of jury foreman died of cancer," NEW YORK TIMES. 23:3, February 23, 1950.

359 "Sheriff says Dr. Sander told him he killed woman in weak moment; hospital librarian testifies," NEW YORK TIMES. 1:6, February 24, 1950.

360 "Sander testimony," NEW YORK TIMES. 30:1, February 25, 1950

361 "Friends and patients of Dr. Sander ask financial aid for defense," NEW YORK TIMES. 51:1, February 26, 1950.

362 "Nurse testifies; husband denies asking Dr. Sander to shorten wife's life," NEW YORK TIMES. 1:2, February 28, 1950.

363 "Fourth witness testifies against Dr. Sander," NEW YORK TIMES. 6:2, March 1, 1950.

364 "Defense plea of somatic death indicated in cross-examination of prosecution witness," NEW YORK TIMES. 5:3, March 2, 1950.

365 "Defense opens case; to hold that patient died before air injections," NEW YORK TIMES. 1:6, March 3, 1950.

366 "500 letters with cash for defense received," NEW YORK TIMES. 19:4, March 3, 1950.

367 "23 defense witnesses express affection for Sander," NEW YORK TIMES. 30:1, March 4, 1950.

368 "$6,000 received for defense," NEW YORK TIMES. 18:3, March 5, 1950.

369 "Reverend C. L. Curtice sermon backs Sander," NEW YORK TIMES. 13:2, March 6, 1950.

370 "Sander denies killing patient; admits air injection; says mind snapped," NEW YORK TIMES. 1:1, March 7, 1950.

CASES OF MERCY KILLINGS

371 "Sander testimony excerpts," NEW YORK TIMES.
    19:1, March 7, 1950.

372 "Dr. R. Ford, Harvard expert testifies that
    air injections did not kill patient,"
    NEW YORK TIMES. 1:6, March 8, 1950.

373 "Sander defense rests," NEW YORK TIMES.
    54:1, March 9, 1950.

374 "Sander acquitted," NEW YORK TIMES. 1:6,
    March 10, 1950.

375 "Editorial - Sander," NEW YORK TIMES. 26:1,
    March 10, 1950.

376 "Sander gets congratulations, N. H. Medical
    Society to consider case," NEW YORK TIMES.
    28:7, March 11, 1950.

377 "Jury foreman says it took more than one
    ballot to acquit," NEW YORK TIMES. 34:2,
    March 12, 1950.

378 "N. H. Medical Society takes no action;
    says county society to which Sander belongs
    must act; N. H. Medical Society comdemns
    euthanasia; State Board of Registration in
    Medicine to fix hearing date," NEW YORK
    TIMES. 23:8, March 13, 1950.

379 "State Board sets Sander hearing date,"
    NEW YORK TIMES. 48:2, March 14, 1950.

380 "2,700 persons contribute $18,000.00 to Dr.
    Sander fund," NEW YORK TIMES. 68:4,
    March 19, 1950.

381 "Hillsborough Medical Society weighs case
    but refuses to comment; Bishop Brady
    scores mercy killing sermon," NEW YORK
    TIMES. 36:8, March 20, 1950.

382 "Two Roman Catholic Hospitals ban Sander;

charges against him filed in Medical Society," NEW YORK TIMES. 22:2, March 21, 1950.

383 "Dr. Sander's license to practice medicine in New Hampshire revoked," NEW YORK TIMES. 1:2, April 20, 1950.

384 "American Academy of General Practice revokes Sander's membership," NEW YORK TIMES. 46:2, April 21, 1950.

385 "Sander expects to resume practice after June 19; license revocation considered, two months suspension," NEW YORK TIMES. 60:3, April 26, 1950.

386 "New Hampshire Attorney General W. L. Phinney who prosecuted Sander resigns post," NEW YORK TIMES. 5:6, April 27, 1950.

387 "Member of medical board which revoked Sander's license reports threatening phone calls," NEW YORK TIMES. April 30, 1950.

388 "Hillsborough County Medical Society drops Dr. Sander," NEW YORK TIMES. 36:4, May 10, 1950.

389 "Sander tills neighbor's soil to support family," NEW YORK TIMES. 29:1, May 14, 1950.

390 "Two nurses at Hillsborough County General Hospital who testified for Sander demoted, one quits," NEW YORK TIMES. 23:7, May 15, 1950.

391 "Dr. Sander quits plowing job as season ends," NEW YORK TIMES. 18:6, May 16, 1950.

CASES OF MERCY KILLINGS

392 "Sander to apply for reinstatement of
      license," NEW YORK TIMES. 29:2, May 19,
      1950.

393 "Dr. H. N. Sander loses plea for readmission
      to Hillsborough (New Hampshire) County
      Medical Society," NEW YORK TIMES. 25:6,
      October 24, 1951.

394 "Sander seeks to regain privilege of using
      Manchester, New Hampshire hospitals - '49
      euthanasia case recalled," NEW YORK TIMES.
      15:6, June 17, 1952.

395 "New Hampshire Medical Society President
      Leivin urges reinstatement in organization,"
      NEW YORK TIMES. 15:1, August 23, 1952.

396 "Hillsborough County (New Hampshire) Medical
      Society again bars reinstatement in mercy
      death case by six votes," NEW YORK TIMES.
      43:2, November 12, 1953.

397 "Sander admitted to Rockingham County (New
      Hampshire) Medical Society by unanimous
      vote," NEW YORK TIMES. 25:6, December 2,
      1954.

398 "Sander reinstated as full member of New
      Hampshire Medical Society," NEW YORK TIMES.
      29:4, December 11, 1954.

SELL: NEWSPAPER ARTICLE

399 "A. J. Sell held for slaying cerebral
      palsied son, 5," NEW YORK TIMES. 1:1,
      March 30, 1953.

SEVIGNY: NEWSPAPER ARTICLES

400 "M. S. Sevigny claims to have poisoned Mrs.
      L. V. Normandin in order to end suffering,"
      NEW YORK TIMES. 8:4, December 17, 1935.
      and 52:3, December 18, 1935.

CASES OF MERCY KILLINGS

401 "Grand Jury refuses to charge nurse, M. Sevigny with murder in alleged mercy killing; says patient died of self-administered poison," NEW YORK TIMES. 3:6, February 1, 1936.

SILVERSTEIN: NEWSPAPER ARTICLE

402 "Mrs. E. Silverstein kills son, P. Loney, Oakland, California," NEW YORK TIMES. 40:2, August 8, 1940.

SOENDERGAARD: NEWSPAPER ARTICLE

403 "Mrs. A. Soendergaard gets probation in killing of 17-year-old son, Copenhagen, Denmark," NEW YORK TIMES. 11:2, February 17, 1950.

STENHOUSE: NEWSPAPER ARTICLE

404 "Father found insane (Joseph Stenhouse); committed to Massillon State Hospital," NEW YORK TIMES. II. 3:4, January 31, 1932.

STEPHENS: NEWSPAPER ARTICLE

405 "J. Stephens, nephew acquitted of mercy slaying," NEW YORK TIMES. 48:6, December 8, 1933.

STEVENS: NEWSPAPER ARTICLE

406 "Dr. J. Stevens kills wife, cancer victim, mongoloid son, then self," NEW YORK TIMES. 35:5, September 23, 1969.

TUTTLE

407 "Potter and euthanasia," TIME. 31:24, January 31, 1938.
    Charles Frances Potter's views concerning euthanasia are discussed. "He would kill for kindness." In addition, the case of

CASES OF MERCY KILLINGS

Dr. Francis A. Tuttle's euthanasia of her ill daughter is examined, with references made to existing policies and laws concerning euthanasia as they exist outside the United States.

UMPLEBY: NEWSPAPER ARTICLE

408 "Pvt. W. Umpleby convicted for killing wife; jury recommends mercy, Leeds, England," NEW YORK TIMES. 9:6, March 20, 1945.

VANDEPUT

409 "Liege verdict," by Right Reverend R. Mortimer. NURSING TIMES. 59:19-20, January 4, 1963.

410 "Mercy killer: legal and moral problems raised by acquittal in murder of thalidomide infant," ECONOMIST. 205:643, November 17, 1962.

The author uses the recent acquittal of Mme. Vandeput and others as a launching point for a discussion of euthanasia. Distinctions between infanticide and man-slaughter are made as well as a prediction of the extent to which British popular sentiment would affect future cases.

411 "No license to kill," SPECTATOR. 289: 744, November 16, 1962.

Is society ready to sanction acts of euthanasia? The issue is discussed with an analysis of the Vandeput acquittal.

412 "Thalidomide homicide," TIME. 80:67, November 16, 1962.

Suzanne Van de Put drugged her thalido-mide baby because of her deformity. This case is reported.

CASES OF MERCY KILLINGS

413 "Tragedy at Liege: Vandeput's thalidomide
        baby - discussion," LOOK. 27:16,
        April 23, 1963.
        Six letters some supporting and some
     condemning the Vandeput's action in the
     mercy killing of their deformed infant
     daughter are presented. One writer
     evokes the "wrath of God" while others
     cry for a "sense of decency" in such
     situations.

NEWSPAPER ARTICLES

414 "Trial opens, Liege, Belgium, of Mrs.
        Vandeput, charged with killing deformed
        thalidomide baby daughter," NEW YORK
        TIMES.
          35:8, November 6, 1962.
          48:1, November 7, 1962.
          47:6, November 8, 1962.
          72:9, November 8, 1962.
          1:7, November 11, 1962.
          59:1, November 11, 1962.
          41:4, November 12, 1962.
          59:5, November 12, 1962.

WARRINER: NEWSPAPER ARTICLE

415 "Warriner reiterates story; killing opposed
        by Dr. T. P. Murdock," NEW YORK TIMES.
        3:6, November 21, 1935.

WASKIN

416 "Mercy killing debated: Chicago Wesley
        Memorial Hospital," AMA NEWS. 10:9,
        August 28, 1967.
        Robert Waskin watched his mother suffer
     through five agonizing hospital stays.
     Because she was in pain and because his
     entire family was suffering great mental
     agony, and acknowledging that his mother
     wished death, he shot and killed her.

CASES OF MERCY KILLINGS

WASKIN: NEWSPAPER ARTICLE

417   "R. Waskin fatally shoots mother, incurably
       ill with leukemia,"   NEW YORK TIMES.
       77:6, August 9, 1967.

WEIMER: NEWSPAPER ARTICLE

418   "Killed by sister, Mrs. R. B. Weimer, to
       'end her grief',"   NEW YORK TIMES.   56:4,
       September 16, 1930.

WRESCHLER: NEWSPAPER ARTICLE

419   "G. Wreschler discovered to have killed
       wife, Catherine, mental trouble sufferer,"
       NEW YORK TIMES.   4:7, November 4, 1938.

ZYGMANIAK: NEWSPAPER ARTICLES

420   "Lester Zygmaniak and Dr. Vincent A. Mon-
       temarano are both charged with committing
       euthanasia,"   THE NATIONAL OBSERVER.
       7/7-6, 1973.

421   "Lester Zygmaniak was acquitted of a first-
       degree murder charge after killing his
       paralyzed brother - follow-up,"   THE
       NATIONAL OBSERVER.   11/17-2, 1973.

       SEE ALSO:
         MONTEMARANO

       CASES OF MERCY KILLINGS
         SEE   ALSO:
           THE LAW AND EUTHANASIA

422   "Alive or dead?"   by T. R. Van Dellen.   ILL-
      INOIS MEDICAL JOURNAL.   132:579, October,
      1967.
         When an individual is breathing via a
      respirator, fed intravenously, circulating
      via a pacemaker is that individual alive?
      The American Electroencephalography So-
      ciety propose five criteria for determina-
      tion of death.

423   "Death as an event: A commentary on Robert
      Morison,"   by Leon R. Kass.   SCIENCE.
      173:698-702, August 20, 1971.
         Discusses such topics as: death con-
      cepts, death as an event, death determina-
      tion, and the ethics of prolonging life.

424   "Death in life,:   by O. T. Bailey.   SCIEN-
      TIFIC MONTHLY.   58:117-128, February,
      1944.
         Death arrives in stages; hence it is
      indispensable to life.   Bailey analyzes
      these statements as well as the physi-
      cal process as it applies to the skin,
      hair, nails, blood and bone.   The per-
      manence of living systems is also dis-
      cussed.

425   "Death: process or event?"   by R. S.
      Morison.   SCIENCE.   173:694-698, August
      20, 1971.
         Morison's discussion of death includes
      such topics as: abstractions that can
      lead to discontinuity; is a re-defini-
      tion of death enough; the value of life
      changes with complex interactions; and
      issues that cannot be settled by abso-
      lute standards.

426   "Definition of irreversible coma as a
      criterion for death,"   JOURNAL OF THE
      AMERICAN MEDICAL ASSOCIATION.   205:337-
      340, August 5, 1968.

427 "Diagnosis of life and death," by C. T.
Reilly. JOURNAL OF THE MEDICAL SOCIETY
OF NEW JERSEY. 66:601-604, November, 1969.
In a discussion of the human animal
all types of death should be considered.
Four topics are discussed in detail:
death determination , the socially dead,
heroic treatments, and the donor selection for organ transplants.

428 "Ethical problems created by hopelessly
unconscious patient--editorial," NEW
ENGLAND JOURNAL OF MEDICINE. 278:1455,
June 23, 1968.
Proposes a definition of death that
could end the medical-legal quagmire
caused by the disagreement between the
medical and legal professions.
SEE ALSO:
"Ethical problems created by the hopelessly unconscious patient," by H. K. Beecher. NEW ENGLAND JOURNAL OF MEDICINE.
278:1425-1430, June 27, 1968.

429 "Euthanasia--an overview for our time,"
CALIFORNIA MEDICINE. 118:55-58, March,
1973.
A report of the California Medical Association Committee for continuing study
of evolving trends in society affecting
life during which multiple aspects of
euthanasia is studied. Such terms as
active, passive, positive and negative
euthanasia are defined. Brain death and
suggested criteria for death determination are examined. An analysis of the
Harvard Committee's recommendations is
included.

430 "In death do all tissues die?" by G. Cag-
netto. LA RIFORMA MEDICA. 39:601-605,
June 25, 1923.

431 "Keeping the patient alive: who decides?
     Growing debate over medical ethics," U. S.
     NEWS AND WORLD REPORT. 72:44-49, May 22,
     1972.
        Staff members of the US NEWS AND WORLD
     REPORT talked with practicing physicians,
     medical scientists, lawyers and legisla-
     tors, sociologists, theologians and lay-
     men concerning the miracles of modern
     medicine. Discussed are measures physi-
     cians should use to prolong the life of
     the terminally ill patient, death deter-
     mination, and when a birth-defective baby
     should be allowed to die. Also the ethics
     of human guinea pigs and organ transplants
     are examined.

432 "Life or death by EEG," by H. Hamlin.
     JOURNAL OF THE AMERICAN MEDICAL ASSOCIA-
     TION. 190:112-114, October 12, 1964.
        Discusses death in relation to brain
     function as measured by the EEG. The
     medicolegal aspects of death determina-
     tion are reviewed.

433 "Life or death: a one man decision?"
     GERIATRICS. 21:240-, June, 1966.
        A synopsis of statements made be Dr.
     William P. Williamson which explains the
     the role of the physician, patient, and
     clergyman in determining the end of a
     life. Discusses the problems encountered
     in death determinations.

434 "Medicine, machines, and the relation to
     the fatally ill," by H. P. Lewis. JOURNAL
     OF THE AMERICAN MEDICAL ASSOCIATION. 206:
     387-388, October 7, 1968.
        Modern medicine with its advanced tech-
     nology has created many moral, ethical, and
     legal questions and problems. Definitions
     of death, extraordinary means, and terminal
     illness are reexamined, as well as a
     summary of modern medical techniques and
     procedures.

435 "On the definition of death: the Swedish
    view," by G. Biorck. WORLD MEDICAL
    JOURNAL. 14:136-139, September-October,
    1969.
        Definitions of medical death and brain
    death are presented. Views of the Roman
    Catholic Church concerning euthanasia and
    the employment of extraordinary means are
    discussed through analyzing the writings
    of Pope Pius XII. An evaluation of a
    euthanasia case is also presented.

436 "Problem of euthanasia," by S. Rudikoff.
    COMMENTARY. 57:62-68, February, 1974.
        The problems of euthanasia--brain death,
    the time of death, patient pressures,
    social attitudes, organ transplantation,
    and many other areas are contemplated.
    The idea of establishing a hostice, or
    place where the dying can receive the
    care and comfort they need, is discussed.
    Many publications dealing with the sub-
    ject of death are cited.

437 "Problematical aspects of the phenomenon
    of death," by H. P. Wasserman. WORLD
    MEDICAL JOURNAL. 14:146-149, September-
    October, 1967.
        In this philosophical study of death
    and dying, Wasserman seeks to define life
    and death. Biologically, the definition
    of death appears to be related to the irre-
    versible loss of neural function. Medical
    education ill prepares the doctor for a
    realistic approach to death. Wasserman
    recognizes that death should be looked
    upon as an inevitable event. Additionally,
    he asserts that medical science should
    develop a program of premortem care which
    provides euthanasia as a means of death
    without suffering.

438 "Problems of euthanasia by S. Rudiskoff -
    discussion," COMMENTARY. 57:7-8 passim,

May, 1974.
A letter to the editor elaborating on
Sonya Rudikoff's article on euthanasia
appearing in COMMENTARY's February issue.
The commentaries focus on definitions of
death and discussions of the term "brain
death".

439   "Resuscitation edict stirs a storm in
      Britain," MEDICAL WORLD NEWS. 8:54,
      October 20, 1967.
      As a result of the "NTBR (not to be
resuscitated) Memorandum" of the Neasden
Hospital in London furor developed. The
memorandum received praise from physicians.
At Massachusetts General Hospital, guidelines were established in determining
when the patient has died. It was
determined that a flat EEG on all leads
for twenty minutes of continuous reading
plus a patient's failure to respond to
sensory and mechanical stimuli indicate
death has occurred.

SEE ALSO: "When to resuscitate," by
Morris Fishbein. MEDICAL WORLD NEWS.
8:140, October 20, 1964.

440   "The right to die: limits of medical re-
      sponsibility in prolonging life," by V.
      J. Collins. JOURNAL OF THE AMERICAN
      ASSOCIATION OF NURSE ANESTHESISTS. 41:27-
      36, February, 1973.
      In a clear and comprehensive manner, Dr.
Collins discusses the gamut of topics
involving euthanasia. Some of the topics
discussed in detail include life -
integration of function, factors determining death, and the proposal of a dying
score that is similar to the newborn
Apgar score. Information concerning the
proper application and interpretation of
the dying score is given in a concise
tabular form.

441 "Right to die with dignity," NEW PHYSICIAN.
     21:173-174, March, 1972.
        To assist the physician in death
     determination, the Harvard Medical School
     has suggested three basic criteria for
     death determination: (1) lack of response
     to any stimuli, (2) no movements or
     spontaneous breathing and (3) no reflexes.

442 "What is death?" by F. J. Ayd, Jr. NEW
     REPUBLIC. 18:286-291, April, 1969.

443 "What is death," by B. M. Newman. SCIENTIFIC
     AMERICAN. 162:336-337, June, 1940.
        Views death as more than just a momentary
     halting of the heartbeat. And when death
     does occur, bodies do not die all over
     at the same time. Moreover, no simple
     death test exists. Such verisimilitudes
     about death are discussed from a scientific
     viewpoint.

444 "What is life? What is death?" TIME.
     87:78, May 27, 1966.
        For years whether or not a person could
     be pronounced dead depended upon whether or
     not the heart had stopped beating. Mechan-
     ical devices are now available to keep such
     processes continuing indefinitely. A
     reevaluation of criteria for certification
     of death is in order.

445 "When are we dead?" ANNALES DE MEDECINE
     LEGALE, DE CRIMINOLOGIE ET DE POLICE
     SCIENTIFIQUE, MEDICINE SOCIALE ET TOXI-
     COLOGIE. 22:53-60, March, 1942.

446 "When do we let the patient die?" ANNALS
     OF INTERNAL MEDICINE. 68:695-700, March,
     1968.
        This editorial classifies dying patients
     into four categories in an effort to
     organize criteria whereby a doctor's best
     judgment can be used in deciding by what
     means and to what extent a life should

be prolonged. Medical criteria necessary to establish death in each category is discussed. Also problems of organ transplants and its role in prolonging life are posed.

DECISIONS AND MEDICAL ETHICS

447 "The attitudes of physicians toward prolonging life," by T. A. Travis. PSYCHIATRY IN MEDICINE. 5:17-26, Winter, 1974.

448 "Dying patient: tackling the new ethical and legal questions," by J. H. Goldberg. HOSPITAL PHYSICIAN. 4:33, 41-45, June, 1968.
    The suggestion is made by the author that there is a time when resuscitative devices should be used and a time when they should not. Goldberg reports current opinion on resuscitative devices currently in use in the treatment of terminally ill patients.

449 "Editorial: physician's ethics and the right to die," NORDISK MEDICIN (Stockholm) 89:97, April, 1974. (Swedish)

450 "Ethical guidelines someday - what about now?" by D. A. Dansak. HOSPITAL PHYSICIAN. 8:21, September, 1972.

451 "Ethical problems created by the hopelessly unconscious patient," by H. K. Beecher. NEW ENGLAND JOURNAL OF MEDICINE. 278: 1425-1430, June 27, 1964.
    One can distill from this article two major conclusions: there comes a time when it is no longer appropriate to continue life by extraordinary means for unconscious patients, and that society can ill afford to discard organs of these patients when they are so greatly needed

by other salvagable patients. Definitions of death are also discussed.

SEE ALSO: NEW ENGLAND JOURNAL OF MEDICINE. 278:1455, June 27, 1968.

452 "Ethics and euthanasia," by Joseph Fletcher. AMERICAN JOURNAL OF NURSING. 73:670-675, April, 1973.

453 "Euthanasia: a growing concern for physicians - interview," by A. Verwoerdt. GERIATRICS. 22:44, 48, 52, passim. August, 1967.
Discusses the opinion of the medical profession to euthanasia; the handling of the subject of euthanasia in the medical schools; societal attitudes toward euthanasia in the United States; instances where euthanasia might be properly used; general guidelines arriving at a euthanasia decision; relationship of medical advances and euthanasia; and euthanasia legislation.

454 "Euthanasia; a problem in medical ethics," by E. F. Torrey. McGILL MEDICAL JOURNAL. 30:127-133, October, 1961.

455 "Euthanasia - the next medical dilemma," by P. R. Gastonguay. AMERICA. 130:152-153, March 2, 1974.

456 "Euthanasia weighed," AMERICAN JOURNAL OF NURSING. 71:359-360, February 1971.
In this abstract of an address given by Dr. Fletcher to the 1970 Conference on Euthanasia, the doctor spoke of three decisive ethical issues - whether quality of life is as important as quantity, whether or not death is a friend, and whether we should make decisions "just".

457 "Euthanasia; who is to judge of the incurability of a disease?" COMMONWEAL.

DECISIONS AND MEDICAL ETHICS

19:215, December 22, 1933.

458 "Extreme measures to prolong life," by
      Very Reverend Brian Whitlow and F. Rosner.
      JOURNAL OF THE AMERICAN MEDICAL ASSOCIATION.
      202:374-376, October 23, 1967.
         An inquiry was given to these two above-
      mentioned authors concerning the use of
      extraordinary means of preserving life in
      terminally ill patients. Reverend
      Whitlow believes that the final decision
      must be made by the physician, and, that if
      he is trying to do the best for the patient
      he is more than likely to follow the proper
      course of action. Dr. Rosner believes that
      no general answer is available. Each case
      must be judged individually; moreover, he
      does not know by whom the judging should be
      done.

459 "Keeping patients alive: who decides? Grow-
      ing debates over medical ethics," U. S.
      NEWS AND WORLD REPORT. 72:44-49, May 22,
      1972.
         Presents a survey conducted by the staff
      of U. S. NEWS AND WORLD REPORT on death,
      euthanasia, and extraordinary means of the
      prolongation of life. Doctors, theologians
      and prominent persons are interviewed.

460 "Life and living it," by Y. Cross, et al.
      NURSING MIRROR AND MIDWIVES JOURNAL.
      133:49-51, October 15, 1971.
         By posing difficult situations which
      require ethical judgment, the doctor
      seeks to discover how others resolve the
      conflicts faced in the medical profession
      today - abortion, euthanasia and organ
      transplantation.

461 "Life-death decisions may undermine M. D.'s
      mental health," by C. K. Hofling. FRON-
      TIERS IN HOSPITAL PSYCHIATRY. 5(5):3,
      March, 1968.

Asserts that decision-making in a case of euthanasia should be a group effort calling upon the expertise of the physician, clergyman, family, and friends.

462 "Life, dying, death: ethics and open decisions," by A. Etzioni. SCIENCE NEWS. 106:109, passim. August 17, 1974.
Etzioni discusses the question of how much effort should be invested in sustaining a dying person or a severely malformed newly-born infant and into whose hands these decisions should be placed. Calls for a grand public debate in order for society to form new ethical criteria on who shall live and when to let someone die.

463 "Life or death," by D. Whitten. TODAY'S HEALTH. 52:48-53, March, 1974.
The subject of bioethics has come to mean all of the social and ethical decisions involved in medicine, including what actions should be taken from what actions can be undertaken. The establishment of ethics rounds for medical students is considered as asset in the training of physicians because it exposes these students to the ethical dilemmas whereby they have time to reflect on the best course of action for the patient. The purpose of these rounds is to broaden the decision making scope of medicine and to supply personnel trained to make value judgments into medical practice.

464 "Life or death: the physician as judge and jury," by Ann Pappert. CANADIAN DOCTOR. 38:66-68, March, 1972.
The problem, with respect to kidney disease, of deciding whose life is to be prolonged by recent advances in dialysis is analyzed.

73

465 "Limits of medical responsibility in prolonging life," by V. J. Collins.
JOURNAL OF THE AMERICAN MEDICAL ASSOCIATION.
206:389-392, October 7, 1968.
Although extraordinary means might be
employed to sustain a human existence,
the quality of this preserved life must
be considered. The primary determinant of
medicine is to insure man's existence as
a whole human being with a meaningful
life. Definitions of euthanasia, aspects
of prolonging life, ordinary and extraordinary means, and effectiveness of
therapy are discussed. Legal, religious,
and secondary responsibilities are also
explained.

466 "Matters of life and death: euthanasia;
resuscitation; treatment of incurables,"
CANADIAN MEDICAL ASSOCIATION JOURNAL.
93(13):718-719, 1965.

467 "May doctors kill?" by Harry Roberts.
LIVING AGE. 347:159-162, 1934.
Dr. Harry Roberts gives his answer to
the question, "May doctors kill?" When
sympathy outweighs the fear of the law,
act upon it. This principle is applicable
to cases where Dr. Roberts admits that he
would not hesitate to painlessly end the
life of a patient suffering from such a
painful disorder as cancer of the larynx;
however, he would also not be an enthusiast
for euthanasia unless such acts were
heavily safeguarded.

468 "Moral tension and an ethical frontier,
death and medical initiative," by J.
Fletcher. CHRISTIAN SCHOLAR. 46:261-
266, Fall, 1963.
A discussion of terms such as voluntary
and involuntary euthanasia is given.
Anti-dysthanasia is proposed. Two tragic
errors in modern medical thinking are

pointed out - vitalism and salubrism.
Mr. Fletcher sites his purpose for writing
this article as a means to challenge the
morality of salubrist vitalism in the
name of freedom and personalism.

469 "The morality of triage," by Thomas J.
O'Donnell. GEORGETOWN MEDICAL BULLETIN.
14:68-71, August, 1960.
The author presents an analysis of pro
and con situations which arise when the
decision either to continue or discontinue
life-sustaining measures for critically
ill patients must be made.

470 "Neasden memorandum on resuscitation,"
BRITISH MEDICAL JOURNAL. 3:858-859,
September 30, 1967.
The Neasden Memorandum states specific
instances where resuscitation is not to
be administered. As a result of this
memorandum, a "Committee on Inquiry" was
called to examine the memorandum and its
implications. Exception is taken to some
points of the memorandum. Also included an
expansion of ideas on the entire matter of
resuscitation.

471 "On the quantity and quality of life -
fruitless longevity," by Perrin H. Long.
RESIDENT PHYSICIAN. 6:69-70, April,
1960.
The author seeks to evoke one's sense
of ethics as medical science endlessly
prolongs fruitless existences. He
suggests that the quality of an existence
is far more important than mere length of
existence.

472 "The prolongation of life," by J. W.
Provonsha. BULLETIN OF THE AMERICAN
PROTESTANT HOSPITAL ASSOCIATION. 35:14-
16, Spring, 1971.

The Christian ethic comes under scrutiny when such questions as, "Shall I do anything to hasten death? and How long shall I keep the patient alive?" are posed. The solution proported here involves two basic points: "agape" love and the method of applying the norm to analyze a specific situation with which one is involved.

473 "Prolongation of life in the incurably ill and dying," by Perrin H. Long. RESIDENT PHYSICIAN. 6:51-53, June, 1960.
It remains the requirement of medical science that a quality of existence be realized. The prolongation of life remains a problem of medical ethics. Perrin suggests that one must consider more than length of existence when treating the terminally ill patient.

474 "Prolongation of life or prolonging the act of dying," by W. P. Williamson and Reverend F. W. Reid, Jr. JOURNAL OF THE AMERICAN MEDICAL ASSOCIATION. 202:162-163, October 9, 1967.
A patient with advanced arteriosclerosis has been in a state of semiconsciousness three months. Her attending physician finds himself in a dilemma as to whether or not the continuation of extraordinary treatment is warranted. The physician posed the question to the staff of the JOURNAL OF THE AMERICAN MEDICAL ASSOCIATION. The results are two opinions - one by Dr. W. P. Williamson, and the other by Fred W. Reid, Jr., a chaplain.

475 "Realities of the responsibility; what are the real priorities in medical and nursing care?" by W. S. Parker. NURSING TIMES. 67:1053-1054, August 26, 1971
The priorities of medical care are examined - illustrated by the grossly handicapped child and the human-vegetable.

Suggests that professional integrity involves more than mere application of a technical skill.

476 "Resuscitation and euthanasia," by B. P. Galbally. THE AUSTRALIAN NURSE'S JOURNAL. 2:26-29, June, 1973.
Medical science now has the ability to technologically create an artificial survival. The physician is expected to carry on resuscitation as long as brain death remains unproven. In treating the patient, distinctions are made between acts of omission and commission; between deliberate actions and crimes of omission. Active euthanasia is regarded legally as murder. Distinctions are made between active and passive behavior. Galbally also discusses the legal implications of terminating resuscitative measures.

477 "Resuscitation: who makes the decision?" NEW PHYSICIAN. 21: 598 passim, October, 1972.

478 "Round table talk about 'the right to die' - physician's ethics - protection that has been a plague. Is there a request for expanded passive euthanasia?" by Y. Karlsson. NORDISK MEDICIN (Stockholm) 89:100-109, April, 1974. (Multilingual)

479 "Should the patient be kept alive?" by W. P. Williamson. MEDICAL ECONOMICS. 44:60-63, January 9, 1967.

480 "Should we let them die?" SATURDAY EVENING POST. 235:10, passim, May 26, 1962.
The toughest decision a doctor can face is the decision of whether or not to delay death when human conscious life cannot be restored when consciousness alone means life to the human person. Such topics as the Hippocratic Oath, the living dead, and

the employment of extraordinary measures
in patients of accidents versus patients
with diseases are discussed.

481 "Terminal illness and resuscitation: a
hospital philosophy," by T. P. Dearlove.
HOSPITAL AND HEALTH ADMINISTRATION.
(Australia) No. 5:2-5, May, 1972.
Suggests that when an effective
resuscitative procedure is available,
medical and nursing staff should be made
aware of situations when and when not
to use such procedures. Additionally,
Dearlove asserts that medical staff should
avoid the misuse of this life-prolonging
device, and hospital policy in the form
of guidance notes should be implemented.

482 "Test if friendship; a short story," by E.
Poehlman. RN. 34:42-43, passim, October,
1971.
A plea for active euthanasia by a patient
and friend poses a threat to a young
nurse's career and challenges her medical
ethics.

483 "Thanatopsis," by C. W. Blaker. CHRISTIAN
CENTURY. 83:1503-1506, December 7, 1966.
This article begins by presenting a
case history of an individual who was
kept alive by machines for eight years.
From this history, Mr. Blaker launches
into a discussion of death, its definition
and the time when "man is justified in
tampouring with the transition between
the two."

484 "To live - to die," by Reverend T. J.
O'Donnell. JOURNAL OF THE AMERICAN MED-
ICAL ASSOCIATION. 228:501, April 22,
1974.
Discusses the place of consent in the
decision not to use extraordinary measures
to prolong life or perhaps drag out the

the process of dying. There are, perhaps, cases where the next of kin may not adequately be able to reflect the wishes of the dying patient. In such cases, the decision making process in determining whether or not to either use or continue extraordinary measures becomes more complex in nature.

485 "To save or let die - the dilemma of modern medicine," by Richard A. Mc Cormick. JOURNAL OF THE AMERICAN MEDICAL ASSOCIATION. 229:172-176, July 8, 1974.
Reflects on the medical dilemmas doctors and parents face when deformed infants face treatment. Advocates for guidelines that may help in decisions about sustaining the lives of grossly deformed and deprived infants. States that it is the task of physicians to provide concrete categories or presumptive biological symptoms for this human judgment.

486 "What is the physician's responsibility toward the hopelessly ill patient whose death is inevitable" - Symposium," PHYSICIANS MANAGEMENT. 11:45-46, May, 1971.

487 "When do we let the patient die?" ANNALS OF INTERNAL MEDICINE. 68:695-700, March, 1968.
This editorial classifies dying patients into four categories in an effort to organize criteria whereby a doctor's best judgment can be used in deciding by what means and to what extent a life should be prolonged. Medical criteria necessary to establish death in each category is discussed. Also, problems of organ transplants and their role in pro- longing life are reviewed.

488 "When should patients be allowed to die? -
     some questions of ethics: symposium,"
     POST-GRADUATE MEDICINE. 43:197-200,
     April, 1958.

     Also continued - 43:222-225, May, 1968.

489 "When to resuscitate," by Morris Fishbein.
     MEDICAL WORLD NEWS. 8:140, October 20,
     1964.
        The decision as to the application of
     life-prolonging efforts remains in the
     hands of the physician. Fishbein suggests
     that resuscitative device implementation
     and euthanasia in any form are in no
     manner related.

     SEE ALSO: "Resuscitation edict stirs a
     storm in Britain," MEDICAL WORLD NEWS.
     8:54, October 20, 1964.

490 "Who shall die?" NEWSWEEK. 70:92, October
     9, 1967.
        Dr. William F. T. Mc Math, superintendent
     of Neasden Hospital, initiated a memorandum
     concerning which patients should and which
     should not be resuscitated. The memorandum
     provoked furor. The case is reported
     briefly as well as views by British and
     American physicians concerning the memo-
     randum.

491 "Who should live?" by G. W. Paulson.
     GERIATRICS. 28:132-136, March, 1973.
        "When the physician holds a patient's
     life in the balance, are heroic efforts
     always justified?" This article reviews
     selected ethical problems in medical
     gerontology, and two representative cases
     emphasize problems related to support of
     life for the aged." (p. 132). On the last
     page of the article are six partial solu-
     tions to some of the ethical dilemmas,
     and they are well worth reading.

DECISIONS AND MEDICAL ETHICS

SEE ALSO:
    EXTRAORDINARY MEANS

EXTRAORDINARY MEANS

492 "AMA discusses death and dignity," HOSPITAL
    SOCIAL WORK DIRECTOR'S BULLETIN. 39:2,
    March-April, 1974.
        The AMA's House of Delegates at the
    American Medical Association in November,
    1973 issued a statement concerning the
    employment of extraordinary means. The
    delegates urged physicians to consult
    and discuss death and aspects of terminal
    illnesses with their patients. The
    delegates asserted that when irrefutable
    evidence exists that biological death is
    imminent, the employment of extraordinary
    means is the decision of the patient and/or
    his family.

493 "The American Medical Association approved
    a guideline saying physicians need not
    use extraordinary means to prolong life
    when there is irrefutable evidence that
    death is imminent: the association con-
    demned euthanasia," THE NATIONAL
    OBSERVER. 12/15-5, 1973.

494 "Artificially prolonging life of patients,"
    by T. W. Duke. MEDICAL RECORD NEWS.
    38:14-15, February, 1967.

495 "Awesome decision to stop heroic measures,"
    by S. Hiscoe. AMERICAN JOURNAL OF NURS-
    ING. 73:291-293, February, 1973.
        A nurse's honest answers to the family
    of a patient whose vegetative life
    would continue with the aid of machines
    helped them arrive at the decision to
    discontinue the use of life-supporting
    measures.

496   "Cancer and conscience,"   TIME.   78:60,
         November 3, 1961.
            Withholding agressive or extraordinary
         treatment to far gone cancer patients
         and telling the patient the truth about
         the diagnosis were subjects of talks
         given at the annual meeting of the American
         Cancer Society in Manhattan.

497   "Court requires extraordinary means to
         prolong life, Miami, Florida,"   HOSPITAL
         PROGRESS.   52:19, August, 1971.
            A Dade County circuit court ruled that
         a physician must use every effort possible
         to sustain life in a terminally ill
         patient.

498   "Editorial: to live - to die,"   JOURNAL
         OF THE AMERICAN MEDICAL ASSOCIATION.   228:
         501, April 22, 1974.
            Discusses the place of consent in
         the decision to use or not to use extra-
         ordinary measures to prolong the life of
         the terminally ill patient.

499   "Ethical problems created by the hope-
         lessly unconscious patient,"   by H. K.
         Beecher. NEW ENGLAND JOURNAL OF MEDICINE.
         278:1425-1430, June 27, 1968.
            One can derive from this article two
         major conclusions: there comes a time
         when it is no longer appropriate to con-
         tinue life by extraordinary means for
         unconscious patients, and that society can
         ill afford to discard organs of these
         patients when they are so greatly needed
         by other salvagable patients. Definitions
         of death are also reviewed.

         SEE ALSO: NEW ENGLAND JOURNAL OF MED-
         ICINE. 278:1455, June 27, 1968.

500   "Extreme measures to prolong life,"   by
         Very Reverend Brian Whitlow and F. Rosner.

JOURNAL OF THE AMERICAN MEDICAL ASSOCIATION.
202:374-376, October 23, 1967.
An inquiry was given to these two above
mentioned authors concerning the use of
extraordinary means of preserving life in
terminally ill patients. Reverend Whitlow
believes that the final decision must be
made by the physician, and that if he
is trying to do the best for the patient,
he is more than likely to follow the
proper course of action. Dr. Rosner
believes that no general answer is available. Each case must be judged
individually; moreover, he does not know
by whom the judging should be done.

501 "Is there not also a spirit?" by A. Bergman. RN. 35:46, May, 1972.
In this short story, concerning a
patient's life unduly prolonged, a nurse
questions whether or not an individual
has the right to die.

502 "It's time to die," NEWSWEEK. 73:90-91,
February 10, 1969.
Whether or not to allow a patient to
die is a tough decision. Two cases are
reported which reveal instances where
the patient sought the removal of extraordinary means; thereby, allowing his
existence to be terminated.

503 "Last illness of Harry Truman," TIME.
101:55, January 8, 1973.
The last fatal illness of President
Harry S. Truman evokes cause for discussion of the prolongation of life by
extraordinary means.

504 "The legal aspects of medical euthanasia,"
by D. W. Meyers. BIOSCIENCE. 23:467-
470, August, 1973.
After an analysis of the implications
of the term, euthanasia, the affirmative

act of causing the death is examined in
detail. Other aspects of euthanasia
such as withholding or terminating
ordinary medical treatment and extraordinary means are discussed.

505 "Legal aspects of the decision not to use
extreme measures to prolong life," by
H. Creighton. SUPERVISOR NURSE. 3:50,
passim, July, 1972.
Helen Creighton's work sites statements by numerous authorities concerning
various aspects of euthanasia and the
various types of death. In her concluding
statements she proposes that it should
be the physician's duty to evaluate
forseeable candidates for cardiac resuscitation and supply specific written orders
as to what means should be employed in
case of heart stoppage. If medical
orders are not available, she believes
that the medical personnel should be
guided by the ethics set forth in this
discussion.

506 "Let the hopelessly ill die?" U. S. NEWS
AND WORLD REPORT. 55:18, July 1, 1963.
A brief analysis of views expressed
by Bishop Fulton J. Sheen on mercy
killing and the employment of extraordinary means is presented. The official
position of the Roman Catholic Church as
of 1957 with regard to euthanasia is
stated.

507 "Machine medicine and its relation to the
fatally ill," by H. P. Lewis. JOURNAL
OF THE AMERICAN MEDICAL ASSOCIATION. 206:
387-388, October 7, 1968.
Modern medicine with its advancing
technology has created many moral, ethical,
and legal questions concerning death.
Definitions of death, extraordinary
means and terminal illness are re-examined

as well as a summary of many modern medical techniques, procedures, and capabilities discussed.

508 "MD's, clergy discuss prolonging life," AMA NEWS. 9:1, passim, May 9, 1966.
Noted authorities, Bishop Fulton J. Sheen, Paul S. Rhoads, Reverend Granger E. Westhrorg and Gotthard Booth discuss the use of extraordinary means to prolong the patient's life. The artificial kidney and artificial heart are two devices specifically discussed. Bishop Sheen discusses the problem in the light of total human life - vegetable, animal and rational. All three stages of existence should be qualitatively maintained through extraordinary treatments, Sheen asserts.

509 "Medical morality: a search for guidelines," JOURNAL OF THE AMERICAN MEDICAL ASSOCIATION. 193:40(Adv), July 12, 1965.
When does one cease the employment of extraordinary means in maintaining an individual's life? And what are the obligations of the physician? These questions are discussed by Reverend Paul B. Mc Cleave, LLD.

510 "No H. P.," by D. P. Trees. JOURNAL OF THE KANSAS MEDICAL SOCIETY. 67:438, August, 1966. (Editorial)
Argues against the employment of extraordinary means. Suggests "no heroics please".

511 "On the treatment of terminal and hopeless patients," ARIZONA MEDICINE. 31:171, March, 1974.
Physicians are urged to review the definitions and their understanding of the terms ordinary and extraordinary means.

512   "Procedures for the appropriate management
      of patients who may have supportive
      measures withdrawn," by H. K. Beecher,
      et al. JOURNAL OF THE AMERICAN MEDICAL
      ASSOCIATION. 209:405, July 21, 1969.
         Once extraordinary means are no longer
      employed, patients must be monitered
      carefully and closely in order to pro-
      vide maximum comfort and to determine
      death.

513   "Prolongation of life or prolonging the
      act of dying," by W. P. Williamson and
      Reverend F. W. Reid, Jr. JOURNAL OF
      THE AMERICAN MEDICAL ASSOCIATION. 202:
      162-163, October 9, 1967.
         A patient with advanced arteriosclerosis
      has been in a state of semiconsciousness
      three months. Her attending physician
      finds himself in a dilemma as to whether
      or not the continuation of extraordinary
      treatment is warranted. The physician
      posed the question to the staff of the
      JOURNAL OF THE AMERICAN MEDICAL ASSOCIATION.
      The results are two opinions by Dr. W. P.
      Williamson, and one by Fred W. Reid, Jr.,
      a chaplain.

514   "To live - to die," by Reverend T. J. O'
      Donnell. JOURNAL OF THE AMERICAN MED-
      ICAL ASSOCIATION. 228:501, April 22,
      1974.
         Discusses the place of consent in the
      decision not to use extraordinary measures
      to prolong life or perhaps drag out the
      process of dying. There are cases, O'-
      Donnell asserts, where the next of kin
      may not adequately be able to reflect
      the wishes of the dying patient. In
      such cases, the question of who is to
      make the decision becomes ever-more
      difficult.

EXTRAORDINARY MEANS

515 "When do we let the patient die?" ANNALS
OF INTERNAL MEDICINE. 68:695-700,
March, 1968.
  This editorial classifies dying patients
into four main categories in an effort
to organize criteria whereby a doctor's
best judgment can be used in deciding by
what means and to what extent a life should
be prolonged. Medical criteria necessary
to establish death in each category is
discussed. Also, problems of organ
transplants and their role in prolonging
life are reviewed.

NEWSPAPER ARTICLE

516 "Dignified death," LOS ANGELES TIMES.
December 5, 1973.
  Discusses the American Medical Association's convention on December 5, 1973 where
euthanasia and extraordinary means were
discussed.

SEE ALSO:
DECISIONS AND MEDICAL ETHICS

517   "The act of dying," by H. Barber.
      PRACTITIONER. 161(962):76-79, August,
      1948.

518   "Address of Dr. D. Marion, director of the
      association," by D. Marion. UNION
      MEDICALE DU CANADA. 79(12):1472-1473,
      December, 1950.

519   "After the Liege lawsuit," SEMAINE DES
      HOPITAUX DE PARIS, INFORMATIONS (Supple-
      ment to SEMAINE DES HOPITAUX DE PARIS).
      5:4-5, January 30, 1963.

520   "Appunti sull' eutanasia," by V. M.
      Palmieri. MINERVA MEDICA (Torino).
      41(38):227-229, July 28, 1950.

521   "Attitudes among clergy and lawyers toward
      euthanasia," by C. E. Preston and J.
      Horton. JOURNAL OF PASTORAL CARE. 26:
      108-115, June, 1972.

522   "Beyond ZPG," by N. Podhoretz. COMMENTARY.
      53:6, May, 1972.
         Mr. Podhoretz warns of dangers that
      could be caused by population control
      movements that try to control not only
      population size but also the character
      and stock through elimination of genet-
      ically imperfect specimens.

523   "Beyond ZPG - reply," by Julius Paul.
      COMMENTARY. 54:22-23, December, 1972.
         The author states his argument with
      the ideaology of ZPG, but he also asserts
      that society must consider its history of
      urgencies and hereditarian attitudes.

524   "Blurring line between life and death,"
      SENIOR SCHOLASTIC INCLUDING WORLD WEEK.
      104:12-14, May 2, 1974.

525   "A case of mercy killing," SVENSKA

LAKARTIDNINGEN. (Stockholm). 61:3619-
3621, November 18, 1964. (Swedish)

526 "Catholic physicians stress respect for
life," HOSPITAL PROGRESS. 51:13-14,
November, 1970.
Declares that every human life must
be unconditionally respected. Suggests
that while the act of euthanasia is a
moral crime, the physician is not
obliged to use every technique known
to medical science to prolong the life
and/or suffering of someone who is
incurable ill.

527 "Changing concepts of death," by John J.
Lowry. HAWAII MEDICAL JOURNAL. 30:
251-257, July-August, 1971.
After a discussion of the idea of death
and on life expectancy, Dr. Lowry
discusses various aspects of death.
Topics in the article include medical
advances, urinary dialysis, transplants,
cerebral death, legal and legislative
action and implications, the right to
refuse treatment, death with dignity
and moral considerations.

528 "Coup de grace - discussion," by W. S.
Hackman. CHRISTIAN CENTURY. 84:20,
January 4, 1967.
Letter from W. S. Hackman concerning
M. Shedeler's "Coup de grace" article.

SEE ALSO: CHRISTIAN CENTURY. 83:1499-
1502, December 7, 1966.

529 "The culprits," by R. A. Montero. ACTA
PEDIATRICA ESPANOLA. (Madrid). 21:82-
86, February, 1963, (Spanish)

530 "Death by chance, death by choice; adaptation of death by choice," by D. C.
Maguire. ATLANTIC MONTHLY. 233:56-65,

June, 1974
"Medicine marches on. The law and ethics straggle behind. We have the knowledge to prolong life. Here, a Catholic theologian asks if we have the wisdom to end it," p. 57.

531 "Death by chance, death by choice; adaptation of death by choice, - discussion," ATLANTIC MONTHLY. 233:26, March, 1974.

532 "Death in incurable disease," INDEPENDENT. 73:1385-1387, December 12, 1912.

533 "Death of a son," by P. D. Sholin. LADIES HOME JOURNAL. 85:68, October, 1968.

534 "Death with dignity," by W. Sachett, Jr. SOUTHERN MEDICAL JOURNAL. 64:330-332, March, 1971.
Presented is a paper read before a meeting of the Southern Medical Association, 1969, in which Sackett proposes to physicians that they permit the hopelessly ill patient to die with dignity and not prolong his life when it has reached an end to its meaningful state. Florida legislation is reviewed.

535 "Death without dignity," TIME. 104:58-59, July 1, 1974.
A review of the ideas and ideals surrounding the primary tenants of the death with dignity standard. Pro and con arguments of euthanasia are presented.

536 "Death's other kingdom," by S. J. Silber. RESIDENT AND STAFF PHYSICIAN. 20:88-91, January, 1974.
States that physicians will do everything they can to maintain the life of the patient no matter what the cost, pain, indignity or discomfort to the patient. Silber asserts that this is cowardice and suggests a re-examination of the role of the physician is now in order.

537 " The dilemmas of euthanasia, editorial,"
by J. A. Behnke. BIOSCIENCE. 23:459,
August, 1973.
   Behnke discusses the complexity of
the issue of euthanasia as well as
abstracts four articles which appear
in this same issue of BIOSCIENCE.

538 "Diminished responsibility," by Glanville
Llewelyn. MEDICINE, SCIENCE AND THE
LAW. 1:41, 1960.

539 "The doctor looks at euthanasia," by
Wolbarst. MEDICAL RECORD. 149:354,
1939.

540 "Doctors and the right to kill," by H.
Roberts. SPECTATOR. 153:123-124, July
27, 1934.

541 "Doctors and the right to kill by H. Roberts
discussion," SPECTATOR. 153:165, 192,
and 226, August 3-17, 1973.

542 "Doctor's job is to extend life," by M.
E. Silverstein. MEDICAL ECONOMICS.
41:71-73, May 18, 1964.

543 "A drama of our time," by C. Koupernik.
CONCOURS MEDICAL. 84:4687-4688, September
8, 1962. (French)

544 "Dying in academe," by N. L. Caroline.
NEW PHYSICIAN. 21:654-657, November,
1972.

545 "Dying in peace," by P. Mauriao. LE
PRESSE MEDICALE. 61:1413, October 31,
1953.

546 "Dying with dignity," by D. Wolft. SCIENCE.
168, 1403, June 19, 1970.
   Calls for more attention to the quality
of life and for an accentuation of the
philosophy of death with dignity.

547 "Dysthanasia. The problem of prolonging
death," by J. Fletcher. TUFTS FOLIA
MEDICA. (Boston) 8:30-35, January-
March, 1962.
Discusses the problem of dysthanasia
as it logically relates to the classical
issue of euthanasia. In this article,
Fletcher reserves the term euthanasia for
the direct induction of death and the
term dysthanasia for the indirect induction
of death.

548 "Easeful death," NURSING TIMES. 67:97,
January 28, 1971.
Presents a synopsis of a British Medical
Association memorandum entitled The
Problem of Euthanasia. The memorandum
is considered a wise and quiet document
that cannot be too highly commended.

549 "Encore l'euthanasia," by H. Planche.
CONCOURS MEDICAL. 73(2):73-74, January
13, 1951.

550 "Errata interpretazione del vocabolo
eutanasia, un referendum indetto in
Inghlterra; la riposta di Giorgio Bernardo
Shaw; la liceita della cosi detta
uccisione miseruordiòsa. Varia," by G.
Bizzarrini. MINERVA MEDICA. 40(59):
634-640, December 1, 1949.

551 "The ethics of euthanasia," by C. Blomquist. SVENSKA LAKARTIDNINGEN. (Stockholm) 60:1601-1620, May 30, 1963.
(Swedish)

552 "La eutanasia," by R. Ciafardo. REVISTA
DE LA ASOCIACION MEDICA ARGENTINA.
(Buenos Aires) 72(12):561-564, December,
1958.

553 "Dell' eutanasia," by B. Coglievina.
GAZZETTA SANITARIA. 18(5):186, September-

October, 1947.

554 "Eutanasia," by A. Ramos Espinosa.
MEDICINA (Mexico). 30(605)77-78,
Supplement, June 10, 1950.

555 "Eutanasiakeskustelu viritetty tampereella-
discussion on euthanasia started in
Tampere," by K. Lakkola. SAERAAHNOITAJA.
8:334-335, May 10, 1968. (Finnish)

556 "Euthanasia," AMERICAN JOURNAL OF DIGESTIVE
DISEASES. 10:199, May, 1943.

557 "Euthanasia," COMMONWEAL. 19:32, November
10, 1933.

558 "Euthanasia," HEALTH. 6:3, June, 1967.

559 "Euthanasia," LANCET. 2:351-352, August
12, 1961.
Several leading publications concerning
euthanasia are discussed along with
their possible shortcomings.

560 "Euthanasia," LIVING AGE. 232:635,
(1901-1902).

561 "Euthanasia," NEW STATESMAN. 31:633-635,
September 1, 1928.

562 "Euthanasia," POPULAR SCIENCE MONTHLY.
3:90-96, 1872.
Criticizes a volume of philosophical
essays by "The Speculative Club" of 1870.
The sixth article in that volume by Samuel
D. Williams on euthanasia is the center of
the criticism.

563 "Euthanasia," ROCKY MOUNTAIN MEDICAL
JOURNAL. 64:34, June, 1967.

564 "Euthanasia," SPECTATOR. 88:175-176,
     February 1, 1902.
     Presented is a series of letters to
     the editor expressing various views on
     the euthanasia controversy. References
     are made to euthanasia legislation,
     euthanasia as it relates to suicide and
     the "Christian ethic".

565 "Euthanasia," by F. E. Akehurst. MONTH.
     73:532, 1891.

566 "Euthanasia," by A. L. Banks. PRACTITION-
     ER. 161:101-107, August, 1948,

567 "Euthanasia," by J. E. Beart. NURSING
     TIMES. 64:1084, August 9, 1968.

568 "Euthanasia," by F. Bordet. PRESSE MED-
     ICALE. (Paris) 70:2022, October 13,
     1962. (French)

569 "Euthanasia," by H. Bouquet. LE MONDE
     MEDICAL. 53:28-30, January-February,
     1943.

570 "Euthanasia," by L. Brock. PROCEEDINGS
     OF THE ROYAL SOCIETY OF MEDICINE. 63:
     659-663, July, 1970.
     At the October 13, 1973 meeting,
     euthanasia legislation from 1936 to
     date was reviewed. Participants pre-
     sented pro and con arguments justificating
     arguments and the desirability of eutha-
     nasia legislation.

571 "Euthanasia," by J. F. Carneiro. BRASIL-
     MEDICO. 69:407-425, July 2-30, 1955.
     (Portuguese)
     The author reviews the problem of
     euthanasia philosophically, romantically,
     rationally, and naturalistically. He
     examines the problem of overcoming pain,
     and explains the catholic attitude.

In the latter part of this article, Carneiro examines medical aspects of the problem of euthanasia as he reviews the medical aspects of various techniques used by physicians.

572 "Euthanasia," by J. Christie. NINETEENTH CENTURY AND AFTER. 148:106-111, August, 1951.

573 "Euthanasia," by Crinquette. JOURNAL DES SCIENCES MÉDICALES DE LILLE. 81:522-526, October, 1963. (French)

574 "Euthanasia," by G. L. Dickinson. LIVING AGE. 248:445-447, February 17, 1906.

575 "Euthanasia," by H. Eshita. JAPANESE JOURNAL OF NURSING. 33:60-61, August, 1969. (Japanese)

576 "Euthanasia," by C. B. Farras. AMERICAN JOURNAL OF PSYCHIATRY. 119:1104, May, 1963.

577 "Euthanasia," by A. Hurst. QUARTERLY REVIEW. 274:319-324, April, 1940.

578 "Euthanasia," by V. Kratochel, et al. CESKOSLOVENSKE ZDRAVOTNICTVI (Praha). 19:483-486, November, 1971. (Czechoslovakian)

579 "Euthanasia," by B. Liber. MEDICAL RECORD. 160:617-618, October, 1947.
    Discusses the compassion a doctor feels as he watches someone die. Suggests that guidelines must be implemented before euthanasia could be legalized. Checks must be built into the system to keep "black-sheep" from abusing the practice.

GENERAL PERIODICAL LITERATURE

580 "Euthanasia," by F. de P. Miranda.
REVISTA MEDICA DE YUCATAN. 25:119-121,
October 31, 1949.

581 "Euthanasia," by C. M. O'Leary. CATHOLIC
WORLD. 62:579, (1895-1896).

582 "Euthanasia," by V. M. Palmier. MINERVA
MEDICA (Supplement). 2:227-229, July 28,
1950.

583 "Euthanasia," by I. M. Rabinowitch and
H. E. Mac Dermott. McGILL MEDICAL JOURNAL.
19(3):160-176, October, 1950.

584 "Euthanasia," by A. V. Serra. JORNAL DO
MEDICO. (Porto) 21(519):38-48, January 3,
1953. (Spanish)
Reviews many aspects of the subject,
siting cases and presenting the Catholic
viewpoint.

585 "Euthanasia," by A. Simili. MINERVA MEDICA.
2:472-489, October 3, 1951.

586 "Euthanasia," by H. L. Stewart. INTER-
NATIONAL JOURNAL OF ETHICS. 29:48-62,
October, 1918.
This historical and somewhat philosophical discourse attempts to disclose
many weak points in arguments both for
and against euthanasia.

587 "Euthanasia," by Luigi Villa. RASSEGNA
CLINICO-SCIENTIFICA DELL INSTITUTO BIO-
CHIMICO ITALIANO. 28(4):99-104, April,
1952. (Italian)

588 "Euthanasia," by H. P. Wassermann. SA:
NURSING JOURNAL. 39:19-21, August, 1969.

589 "Euthanasia," by H. Wijnbladh. NORDISK
MEDICIN. (Stockholm) 72:1050-1051,
September 3, 1964. (Swedish)

590   "Euthanasia: a physician recalls an in-
        curable case," SPECTATOR. 165:166,
        August 16, 1940.

591   "Euthanasia - a poem," by C. F. Alexander.
        DUBLIN UNIVERSITY MAGAZINE. 40:478-487,
        October, 1852.
            Refers to the happy death of a young
        and gifted lady.

592   "Euthanasia - a poem," by Alfred Austin.
        TEMPLE BAR. 3:472, 1861
            Demands patience upon the part of the
        individual anxiously waiting for death
        to arrive. States that death will come
        in its due course.

593   "Euthanasia: an account of the Council
        for International Organizations of Med-
        ical Sciences round table," by J.
        Joncherer. WORLD MEDICAL JOURNAL. 21:
        63-65, July-August, 1974.
            Describes the purposes and creation
        of CIOMS - Council for International
        Organizations of Medical Sciences.
        Distinguishes three categories according
        to whether medical action is intrinsically
        involved, not intrinsically involved or
        is involved in a mixed situation

594   "Euthanasia: an overview for our time,"
        CALIFORNIA MEDICINE. 118:55-58, March,
        1973.
            A report of the CMA - California Medical
        Association - Committee for Continuing
        Study of Evolving Trends in Society
        Affecting Life, during which multiple
        aspects of euthanasia were discussed.
        Such terms as active, passive, positive,
        and negative euthanasia are expounded upon.
        Death, brain death, and suggested criteria
        for death determination are examined.
        Included is an analysis of the Harvard
        Committee's recommendations. Dictionary-

type definitions are used. Analyzes the
treatment of the concept of death with
dignity.

595   "Euthanasia - an overview of our time -
       editorial," CALIFORNIA MEDICINE. 118:
       38, March, 1973.

596   "The euthanasia and automathanasia con-
       cepts," by Monnerot-Dumaine. PRESSE
       MEDICALE. (Paris) 72:1458-1460, May
       16, 1964. (French)

597   "Euthanasia and death," by Reverend G.
       Gariepy. CATHOLIC HOSPITAL. (Canada)
       2:131-133, March-April, 1974.
         The purpose of this analysis is to
       examine euthanasia and death, their
       implications, the guidelines taught by
       the Catholic Church in relation to these
       issues, and the practical problems
       which are encountered by a patient, his
       family and various health professionals.

598   "Euthanasia and humanism," by K. Winter.
       ZEITSCHRIFT FUR AERZTLICHE FORTBILDUNG.
       (Jena) 68:57-58, January 15, 1974.
       (German)

599   "Euthanasia and the notion of death with
       dignity," by R. M. Cooper. CHRISTIANITY
       TODAY. 90:225-227, February 21, 1973.
         Emphasis in this article lies with the
       concept of human dignity. While chosing
       to explain the phrase "death with dignity,"
       the author seeks to define a dignified
       death encompassing both the concepts of
       pleasure and pain. The basic argument
       of the article is best states in this
       sentence: "The evil greater than pain is
       to deny that pain is radically an in-
       gredient of the human condition. "

600   "Euthanasia and the physician," by L.

Derobert. BELGISCH TIJDSCHRIFT VOOR
GENEESKUNDE. (Louvain) 7(15):682-697,
August 1, 1951. (German)

601 "Euthanasia (apropos of a case)," by F.
Loo, et al. ANNALES MEDICO-PSYCHOLGIQUES.
(Paris) 2:465-488, November, 1973.
(French)

602 "Euthanasia by omission," by L. Lattes.
ACTA MEDICINAE LEGALIS ET SOCIALIS.
(Bruxelles) 5(1-2):81-90, January-
June, 1952. (French with English summary)
The question of the allowance of
euthanasia by omission was put to the
Academy. Lattes muses over the question
of the ethicability of prolonging life
in all instances.

603 "Euthanasia creed," by H. Ellis.
SPECTATOR. 155:809-810, November 15,
1935.

604 "Euthanasia doctrine," by G. Bosch.
REVISTA DE MEDICINE LEGAL Y JURISPRUDENCA
MEDICA. 2:171-176, April-June, 1936.

605 "Euthanasia; from the notebook of an
Alpinist," by G. L. Dickinson. IN-
DEPENDENT REVIEW. 7:476, 1905.
Reflections on life and death by
an Alpinist taking place in the Hut and
on the summit.

Also in: LIVING AGE. 248:445, (1905-06)

606 "Euthanasia in England; a growing storm,"
AMERICA. 122:463, May 2, 1970.

607 "Euthanasia in the public interest," by H.
E. de Vries-Kouwenhonen. TIJDSCHRIFT
VOOR ZIKKENVORPLEGING. 27:265-268,
March 19, 1974. (Dutch)

608   "Euthanasia: medical viewpoint,"   by A.
      Casiello.   DIA MEDICO (Buenos Aires)
      33:3061-3066, December 21, 1961.
      (Spanish)

609   "Euthanasia: murder or mercy,"   by A.
      Kent Mac Dougall.   HUMANIST.   18:38-47,
      January-February, 1958.

610   "Euthanasia once more.   INDEPENDENT.   60:
      291-292, February 1, 1906.

611   "Euthanasia or death as a creative process -
      the real question,"   HOSPITAL (Canada).
      2:152-154, May-June, 1974.

612   "Euthanasia or death by pity,"   by C. P.
      Delhaye.   UNION MEDICALE DU CANADA.
      (Montreal)   90:613-622, June, 1961.
      (French)

613   "Euthanasia: right or wrong - discussion,"
      SURVEY GRAPHIC.   37:330, July, 1948.
         Readers' opinions concerning an article
      entitled: "Euthanasia: right or wrong,"
      which appeared in SURVEY GRAPHIC.   37:
      241-243, May, 1948.

614   "Euthanasia society,"   ROCKY MOUNTAIN
      MEDICAL JOURNAL.   69:37, November, 1972.

615   "Euthanasia society exploits news,"
      MEDICAL ECONOMICS.   27(9):111-115, June,
      1950.

616   "Euthanasia sophism,"   by C. Machado.
      PUBLICACOS MEDICAS.   26:241-248, 1956.
      (Portuguese)

617   "Euthanasia? the issue's core,"   by G.
      A. Coe.   RELIGIOUS EDUCATION.   47:168-
      169, March, 1952.

618 "Euthanasia to set you straight," by Carol
O. Rice. MINNESOTA MEDICINE. 49:1269,
August, 1966.
"The primary responsibility of the
physician is to administer to his patient.
It is not to prolong suffering. It is
not to snatch someone from his grave.
Doctors do what any Good Samaritan would
do: they show mercy and compassion,"p.
1269.

SEE ALSO: Elizabeth Davenport in VOGUE.
June, 1966.

619 "Euthanasia? Yes, but what kind?" by A.
F. Schiff. MEDICAL ECONOMICS. 47:259,
passim, May 25, 1970.

620 "Euthanasia - yesterday and tomorrow; an
address," by H. J. Blackman. PLAIN
VIEW. 13:22-32, May, 1960.

621 "Euthanasia," SCALPEL (Bruxelles). 103:
1201-1202, November 18, 1950.

622 "L'euthanasie," by E. Daubresse. SCALPEL.
(Bruxelles) 106(14):365-371, April 4,
1953.

623 "L'euthanasie," by M. De Laet. BRUXELLES-
MEDICAL. 30(53):2747-2751, December 31,
1950.

624 "L'euthanasie," by J. Girard. REVUE MED-
ICALE DE NANCY. 76:329-344, June 1-15,
1951.

625 "Les euthanasies," by C. Simonin. MEDECIN
FRANCAIS. 11(3):63-64, March, 1951.

626 "Euthanasie, dysthanasie, orthothanasie,"
by R. Led. SCALPEL. (Bruxelles) 104(2):
54, January 13, 1951.

627   "Das euthanasieproblem," by H. D. Ditfurth
        DEUTSCHE RUNDSCHAU. 76:348-355, May,
        1950. (German)

628   "The face of death - a poem," by Audrey
        Wurdemann. FORUM. 95:41, January, 1936.

629   "Freedom to die," by F. Canavan. AMERICA.
        110:33, January 11, 1964. (Satire)

630   "Good and bad death," by L. Lattes.
        MINERVA MEDICA. 44(27):847-854, April 4,
        1953.

631   "A good death: increasing support for
        euthanasia spurs heated medical debate,"
        by Ellen Graham. THE WALL STREET JOURNAL.
        179:1, passim, January 31, 1972.

632   "Grandpa's grandpa," by W. C. Bornemeler.
        JOURNAL OF THE OKLAHOMA STATE MEDICAL
        ASSOCIATION. 61:51, passim, February,
        1968.
           "Today's goal - prolonging life - may
        be tomorrow's ethical quagmire. A
        Chicago surgeon tells a tale about how
        a lad, yet unborn, might discuss his
        grandpa's grandpa's death in the family."
        p. 51. (Fiction)

633   "Have we the right to prolong dying?" by
        F. R. Ruff. MEDICAL ECONOMICS. 37:38,
        passim, November 7, 1960.

634   "Health, science and the social conscience,"
        by L. F. Detwiller. HOSPITAL ADMINISTRA-
        TION IN CANADA. 7:38-39, June, 1965.

635   "Health services or sickness services?"
        by E. Slater. BRITISH MEDICAL JOURNAL.
        4:734-736, December 18, 1971.
           Eliot Slater presents a basic discussion
        of such topics as perinatal risks; life

saving or death prevention, and accepted
tradition. The center of thought is devoted to the good life--not just meager
existence.

636 "Help for the living, help for the dying
and euthanasia," by P. Sporken. TIJD-
SCHRIFT VOOR ZIEKENVERPLEGING. 25:305-
311, March 28, 1972. (Dutch)

637 "The hopeless case," by E. G. Laforet.
ARCHIVES OF INTERNAL MEDICINE. 112:314-
326, September, 1963.

638 "Hopelessly unconscious patient," by A.
Moraczewski and J. Adriant. POSTGRADU-
ATE MEDICINE. 44:126-129, December, 1968.

639 "How do you stand?" by D. Sales. AORN
JOURNAL. 6:40-, October, 1967.

640 "Human drama in death and taxes; murder
incorporated," by J. Fisher. TRUST AND
ESTATES. 112:428-429, June, 1973.

641 "Human rights, human dignity and euthanasia,"
by H. Weise. DEUTSCHES ZENTRALBLATT FUR
KRANKENPFLEGE. 11:10-14, January, 1967.
(German)

642 "Interpreted letter: Euthanasia Act," LAN-
CET. 2:39, July 3, 1971.
Dealing with the family of a potential
euthanasia participant can be difficult,
disconcerting and painful. Such a doctor-
patient-family relationship is discussed
in this tightly composed, point-well-taken
letter.

643 "Is euthanasia christian?" by E. N. Jackson.
CHRISTIAN CENTURY. 67:300-301, March 8,
1950.
Divided into four sections, and the medical, theological and legal aspects of euthanasia are discussed.

644 "Is mercy killing justified?" by A. A. Brill.
VITAL SPEECHES. 2:165-167, December 16,
1935.

645 "It's illegal to die," SCIENCE DIGEST. 74:
52, December, 1973.

646 "Last rights," by M. Mannes. FAMILY HEALTH.
6:24-25, 44-45, January, 1974.

647 "Last rights, by M. Mannes--Review," NEW
REPUBLIC. 170:27-28, March 2, 1974.

648 "Legalize euthanasia," by Wolbarst. THE
FORUM. 94:330-332, 1935.

649 "Let them die with dignity," by J. Chernus.
MEDICAL ECONOMICS. 41:65-71, May 18, 1964.

650 "Let the dying die," by P. Moor. SATURDAY
EVENING POST. 239:12-, September 12, 1966.

651 "Let the hopelessly ill die?" by U. S. NEWS
AND WORLD REPORT. 55:18, July 1, 1963.
A brief analysis of views expressed by
Bishop Fulton J. Sheen on mercy killing
and the employment of extraordinary means
is presented. The official position of
the Catholic Church as of 1957 with regard
to euthanasia is stated.

652 "Let's respect death, too," JOURNAL OF THE
KANSAS MEDICAL SOCIETY. 69:328, June, 1968.
A reprint of an article which appeared
in the IOLA REGISTER April 26, 1968 telling
of the plight of the parents of a 13 year
old boy who suffered total brain damage as
the result of an accident. Discusses the
ideas presented as a possible solution, and
also presents arguments for compassion.

653 "Life and death," by W. H. Dempsey. COM-
MONWEAL. 80:156-157, April 24, 1964.

Reviews a book entitled, The Right to Life, by Norman St. John-Stevas. (Holt, Rinehart and Winston, 1964).

654 "Life at everyone's cost?" by A. de Gier. TIJDSCHRIFT VOOR ZIEKENNERPLEGING. 25: 293-294, March 28, 1972. (Dutch)

655 "Life, death, dignity and doctors," by F. B. Berry. RESIDENT AND STAFF PHYSICIAN. 17:14-, October, 1971.

656 "Life or death--whose decision?" by W. P. Williamson. JOURNAL OF THE AMERICAN MEDICAL ASSOCIATION. 197:793-795, September 5, 1966.
Suggests that there exists a grave difference between murder and euthanasia, but not between active and passive euthanasia. Dr. Williamson analyzes the euthanasia controversy by discussing the churches positions and extraordinary and ordinary means.

657 "A life prolonging treatment interrupted," by A. Henriques. SVENSKA LAKARTIDNINGEN. Stockholm. 60:1643-1644, May 30, 1963. (Swedish)

658 "Limits of the life preservation of internal medicine," by J. Koller. PRAXIS. 61: 1259-1263, October 10, 1972. (German)

659 "Malthus, morality and miracle drugs," by E. Shanbrom. JOURNAL OF THE AMERICAN MEDICAL ASSOCIATION. 182:856-857, November 24, 1962.
Discusses Darwin's law of survival of the fittest and natural selection. States that with the increased use of antibiotics, physicians have not allowed nature to take its course. The result has been an increase in the number of aged and infirmed. The primary issue is not whom shall we kill but who shall we let live.

660 "Medicina e eutanasia," by L. Portes. JOR-
NAL DO MEDICO. (Porto). 16(392):155-
162, July 29, 1950.

661 "Medicine and euthanasia, by L. Portes.
BULLETIN DEL ORDRE DES MEDECINS. 85-100,
March, 1951.

662 "Medicine et euthanasie," by R. Laulan.
MERCURE DE FRANCE. 307:356-358, October,
1969. (French)

663 "Medicine, law and human life: 3rd World
Congress on Medical Law," WORLD MEDICAL
JOURNAL. 21:65, July-August, 1974.
A brief report of a session on eutha-
nasia held by the 3rd World Congress on
Medical Law is given. The moral, ethical,
legal, and historical issues of euthanasia
are studied.

664 "Merciful and pseudo-merciful homicide. Puni-
shable psychogenesis and differential
diagnosis," by E. F. Bonnet. PRESNA
MEDICA ARGENTINA. (Buenas Aires). 58:
2152-2167, December 31, 1971. (Spanish)

665 "Merciful killing," LITERARY DIGEST. 98:
17, July 21, 1928.

666 "Mercy death," HYGEIA. 25:976-, December,
1947.

667 "Mercy killing," BRITISH JOURNAL OF NURSING.
95:85, July, 1950.

668 "Mercy killing," SCHOLASTIC-SENIOR. 55:
13, January 11, 1950.

669 "Mercy killing issue--and one more pill,"
ROCKY MOUNTAIN JOURNAL. 65:38, January,
1968.

670 "Mercy murders once more: euthanasia,"

COMMONWEAL. 12:293, July 16, 1930.

671 "Mr. Tollemache on the right to die," THE
SPECTATOR. 46:206-, 1873.
The author discovers that the strongest
arguments for putting an end to human
suffering apply to cases where one cannot possibly have the consent of the
sufferer.

672 "Modified euthanasia," TIME. 76:38, July 4,
1960.

673 "Moral, religious, national, and legal
responsibilities of physicians," by P.
H. Long. RESIDENT AND STAFF PHYSICIAN.
6:53-61, May, 1960.

674 "Morality of breath," by J. Schaefer.
INHALATION THERAPY. 15:79-82, June, 1970.

675 "Murder or mercy," NEWSWEEK. 51:56, February 3, 1958.
Analyzes the difficulties in determining
whether euthanasia is an act of mercy or
an act of murder. The terms are defined.

676 "Napoleon and euthanasia," by C. Brisard.
ANNALES DE MEDECINE LEGALE ET DE CRIMINO-
LOGIE POLICE SCIENTIFIQUE ET TOXICOLOGIE.
32(3):203-208, May-June, 1952. (French)

677 "Natural euthanasia," by B. W. Richardson.
POPULAR SCIENCE MONTHLY. 8:617-620, 1869.
Natural euthanasia, the purely painless
process, occurs as an unconscious passage
into oblivion. Euthanasia, in this form,
is the sequel to health, the happy death
engrafted on the perfect life. Richardson continues and concludes by asserting
that death, as a part of the scheme of
life, is ordained upon the natural term
of life.

678 "Neither life nor death," by L. M. Miller.
     READER'S DIGEST. 77:55-59, December, 1960.
        Voices arguments against not only active
     euthanasia, but also dysthanasia--a delib-
     erate postponement of a merciful death.
     She believes that the dying should be
     allowed to depart in peace, and that those
     doctors, whose interference only prolongs
     the dying process, are doing a grave in-
     justice to the patients under their care.

679 "Notes on euthanasia," by V. M. Palmieri.
     RASSEGNA DI NEUROPISCHIATRIA. 4(6): 607-
     613, November-December, 1950. (Italian)

680 "On direct euthanasia and thanatology," by
     C. Blomquist. SVENSKA LAKARTIDNINGEN.
     60:3788-3799, December 11, 1963. (Swedish)

681 "On the boundary of life.." by N. R. Blume.
     SVENSKA LAKARTIDNINGEN. 60:1640-1642,
     May 30, 1963. (Swedish)

682 "On the definitions of death: the Swedish
     view," by G. Biorck. WORLD MEDICAL
     JOURNAL. 14:136-139, September-October,
     1967.
        Discusses such topics as medical
     death and brain death. Church doctrinal
     views as expressed by Pope Piux XII are
     discussed.

683 "On the problem of euthanasia," by A.
     Hottinger. HIPPOKRATES. 33:815-817,
     October 15, 1962. (German)
        Reviews the book, Borderline Situations
     of Life, by W. Catel.

684 "On the quantity and quality of life," by
     P. H. Long. MEDICAL TIMES. 88:613-619,
     May, 1960.
        Covers moral, legal and religious
     responsibilities of the physician as such
     responsibilities relate to the care of the

incurably ill or dying patient.

685 "Opiniones sobre la eutanasia," MEDICINA
    REVISTA MEXICANA. 31(624):41-44, March
    25, 1951.

686 "Patient's right to die," by J. Fletcher.
    HARPER'S MAGAZINE. 221:138-143, October,
    1960.
       Mr. Fletcher confronts some of the
    issues which sometimes perplex the
    ministry regarding euthanasia. The
    article is divided into three sections: I
    vegetable or human; II medical morals and
    civil law; III the vitalist fallacy.

687 "Patient's right to live and die," by J.
    Beavan. NEW YORK TIMES MAGAZINE. 14,
    passim, August 9, 1959.

688 "Person's right to die," by L. Lasagna.
    JOHNS HOPKINS MAGAZINE. 19:34, passim,
    Spring, 1968.

689 "Les pestiferes de Saint Jean-d'Arc et de
    Jaffa," by E. Forgue. MERCURE DE
    FRANCE. 280:476-497, December 15, 1937.
    (French)

690 "Physicians at bedside of incurable patient,"
    by H. R. Box. NEDERLANDS TIJDSCHRIFT
    VOOR GENEESKUNDE. 100:2601-2610, September
    8, 1956. (Dutch)

691 "Physician, clergyman and patient in
    terminal illness," by E. G. Harris.
    PENNSYLVANIA MEDICAL JOURNAL. 54:541-
    545, June, 1951.

692 "Physiologic bases of natural euthanasia,"
    by F. K. Walter. MUNCHENER MEDIZINISCHE
    WOCHENSCHRIFT. 72:844-846, May 22, 1925.

       Also abstract in: JOURNAL OF THE AMERICAN

MEDICAL ASSOCIATION. 85:314, July 25, 1925.

693 "Der physiologische mechanismus beim tod durch phyischen shock," by G. K. Stureys. KLINISCHE WOCHENSCHRIFT. 21:245-247, March 14, 1942.

694 "Predilection to death," by Avery D. Weisman and Thomas P. Hackett. PSYCHOSOMATIC MEDICINE. 23(3):232-256, 1961.
    Analyzes aspects of the dignified death and the dying patient's attitude toward such a death. Asserts that the dying patient can be reconciled to death when viewing it from this perspective.

695 "Pre-med students meet the pros: seminar held on right to die," by Lester Hieft. PENNSYLVANIA MEDICINE. 75:20-21, Spetember, 1972.
    Presents basic arguments for the popularity of the subject of euthanasia and gives reasons why the subject should be discussed and tells who is currently discussing euthanasia.

696 "Problem in the meaning of death," by Leon R. Kass. SCIENCE. 170:1235-1236, December 11, 1970.
    Medical science has progressed to a state where its ability to prolong life seems indefinite. At an AAAS Symposium, the ability of the physician to maintain a "quality existence" was studied.

697 "The problem of euthanasia," by A. Oraison. MARCO MEDICAL. (Casablanca) 39:321-330, March, 1960. (French)

698 "Problem of euthanasia," by C. J. Reynolds. ENGLISH REVIEW. 51:634-638, November, 1930.

699 "The problem of euthanasia considered by a
    Catholic physician," by P. R. Archam-
    bault. UNION MEDICALE DU CANADA.
    (Montreal) 91:543-546, May, 1962.
    (French)

700 "The problem of life prolonging treatment in
    hopeless cases - from the work of the
    Disciplinary Commission," SVENSKA LAKAR-
    TIDNINGEN. (Stockholm) 60:1635-1640,
    May 30, 1963. (Swedish)

701 "Problem of social control of congenital
    defective; education, sterilization,
    euthanasia," by F. Kennedy. AMERICAN
    JOURNAL OF PSYCHIATRY. 99:13-16, July,
    1942.

702 "Le probleme de l'euthanasia (the problem
    of euthanasia)," by G. Duhamel. FRANCE
    ILLUSTRATION. 6:195, March 4, 1950.
    (French)

703 "Prolongation of dying," by T. H. Gillison.
    LANCET. 2:1327, December 22, 1962.
        Mr. Gillison, in response to an editorial
    of December 8, 1962, argues that the
    exchange of roles by physicians, from
    preservers of life to destroyers, need
    not cause the public to develop undue
    anxiety.

704 "Prolongation of life," by N. Lappin.
    AUSTRALIAN NURSES JOURNAL. 2:21, November,
    1973.

705 "Prolonging life," by G. P. Fletcher.
    WASHINGTON LAW REVIEW. 42:999-1000, 1967.

706 "Prolonging life (4) Nurse's burden, doc-
    tor's decision," by J. Pells. NURSING
    TIMES. 70:393-394, March 14, 1974.
        Jeanne Pells believes that nurses must
    voice their thoughts when faced with

morally questionable situations. However, she also believes that nurses should be in possession of all the available facts before they do any condemning of the medical staff's actions in these questionable cases. A case of the third birth of a spina bifida baby to a mother is one questionable situation which is examined in this article.

707 "Prolonging life (5) Opinions and guidance," by Jeanne Pells. NURSING TIMES. 70: 440-441, March 21, 1974.
In deciding whether to prolong an existence, the patient's age and general condition; the nature of his disease; the availability and practicability of means of cure or relief; and his own wishes and beliefs must collectively be considered by the physician. Other considerations proported by Ms. Pells are the good of society and codes of ethics. "Conscience is our inborn thermostat for right and wrong ... if you hesitate, don't do it." (p. 441)

708 "Prolonging life - the hope in experiment - part 3," by Jeanne Pells. NURSING TIMES. 70:352-353, March 7, 1974.
Pells continues her discussion of the dangers which one encounters in experimental surgery, abortion, and euthanasia. She expounds on the "geriatric argument" and examines euthanasia and abortion legislation.

709 "The quality of death - editorial," WORLD MEDICAL JOURNAL. 21:61-62, July-August, 1974.
Summarizes views concerning euthanasia that were presented by members of the Third World Congress on Medical Law held in Gent. A copy of the "Living Will" document is included.

GENERAL PERIODICAL LITERATURE

710 "Question of love and death: a school
      dramatization," by A. Rubin. SENIOR
      SCHOLASTIC INCLUDING WORLD WEEK. 104:6-
      10, May 2, 1974.
        A three act play, a school dramatization,
      portrays the human dilemma that the parents
      of a badly burned son must face in decid-
      ing his fate.

711 "Question of real or apparent death: modern
      problem," by A. Daniel. ANNALES DE
      HYGIENE PUBLIQUE, INDUSTRIELLE ET SOCIALE.
      18:100-116, March, 1940.

712 "Rcn representative body meeting, Harrogate.
      Nurses at war," NURSING TIMES. 65:1400-
      1401, October 30, 1969.
        The policy resolution on euthanasia
      that was presented at the Rcn meeting
      was carried with only five against and
      ten abstentions. Details of the resolution
      are not discussed in this article. Also,
      a call was made for abortion units to be
      set up, and this resolution was carried.

713 "Reflections on euthanasia," by Vejar
      Lacane, C. GACETA MEDICA DE MEXICO.
      93:817-828, September, 1963. (Spanish)

714 "Reprints of the National Observer story,
      Why prolong life?, are available," THE
      NATIONAL OBSERVER. 3/18-1, 1972.

715 "Resuscitation of patients after cardiac
      arrest: report of Committee of Inquiry,"
      NURSING TIMES. 63:1295, September 29,
      1967. Also editorial. 63:1293-1294,
      September 29, 1967.

716 "Right to die," SPECTATOR. 185:603,
      December 1, 1950.

717 "Right to die," by C. Bavin. SPECTATOR.
      184:466, April 7, 1950.

718 "Right to die," by J. Bovel. WISCONSIN
MEDICAL JOURNAL. 73:9-10, August, 1974.
Takes the position that individuals
have an inherent right to die with a
certain amount of dignity. The circumstances surrounding Sigmund Freud's death
are used in illustrating the author's
position.

719 "The right to die," by Selig Greenberg.
PROGRESSIVE. 30:37-40, June, 1966.
Greenberg discusses the voluntary
aspects of euthanasia as well as implications of "the right to prolong life".

720 "Right to die," by S. L. Henderson Smith.
LANCET. 2:1088-1089. November 21, 1970.
Underlines the fact that attitudes
toward death are entrenched in irrational
fear and prejudice. Suggests that what
is needed is a new philosophy of death
so that death no longer appears as the
worst of all choices.

721 "The right to die," by J. T. Schreuder.
TIJDSCHIRFT VOOR ZIEKENVERPLEGING. 25:
295-299, March 28, 1972. (Dutch)

722 "Right to die," by D. Shields. RN. 27:
80, passim, May, 1964.

723 "Right to die?" by J. Sinton. NURSING
MIRROR AND MIDWIVES JOURNAL. (England)
139:41, July 26, 1974.
Advocates euthanasia by choice by
insisting that human dignity necessitates
freedom of choice in dying.

724 "Right to die," by S. L. Smith. LANCET.
2:1249, December 12, 1970.
This letter is a brief argument on
Dr. Vere's choice of words ... "right"
for "option".

725 "Right to die - discussion," ATLANTIC
    MONTHLY. 221:34-36, June, 1968.
       Ten letters discussing the right to
    die are presented. Various attitudes,
    arguments, and concepts are revealed.
    Views range from positions taken upon
    euthanasia as it relates to mongolism
    to Christian ethics.

726 "Right to die - discussion," SPECTATOR.
    184:500-538, passim, April 14-18, 1950.

727 "Right to die - opinion of physicians,
    church-men and press," LITERARY DIGEST.
    120:17, November 23, 1935.
       The issue of whether or not an
    individual racked in pain from an incurable
    illness can chose to mercifully end his
    life is the subject of the controversy.
    Various viewpoints are presented in this
    article.

728 "Right to die - reply," by J. M. Merriman.
    SPECTATOR. 185:734, December 22, 1950.

729 "Right to die with dignity," by J. G.
    Zimring. NEW PHYSICIAN. 23:52-53,
    April, 1974.

730 "Right to kill," SPECTATOR. 143:654,
    November 9, 1929.

731 "Right to kill," by W. W. Gregg. NORTH
    AMERICAN REVIEW. 237:239-249, March,
    1934.
       Discusses euthanasia (active and passive),
    abortion, infanticide, and capital punish-
    ment. Legal and moral implications are
    analyzed as the author discusses the
    sacredness of life.

732 "The right to kill," by L. Ruppel.
    COLLIER'S. 125:13, April 22, 1950.

The editor explains why he reprinted
an article entitled, "Euthanasia: to be
or not to be". Reference is made to the
Sander trial, and to the acuteness of
euthanasia as a current medical problem.

733 "The right to live," by Rowe. RN. 28:
72, passim, May, 1965.

734 "Right to live and the right to die," by
E. A. Stead, Jr. RESIDENT PHYSICIAN.
14:62-66, March, 1968.

735 "Right to painless death," by R. F.
Rottary. QUARTERLY REVIEW. 274:39 49,
January, 1970.

736 "The rule on euthanasia is impossible,"
by L. Eitinger. NORDISK MEDICIN. 89:
168, June, 1974. (Norwegian)

737 "Sacrification individuelle des petits
animaux. (euthanasia for animals).
BULLETIN DE L'ACADEMIE VETERINAIRE DE
FRANCE. 14:67, 1941. (French)

738 "Science, religion and moral judgment,"
by E. W. Barnes. NATURE. 166:455-457,
September 16, 1950.
Biship Barnes discusses the possible
role of euthanasia as a solution to some
of the world's problems, such as, its
role in capital offenses, in the eradication of abnormal genes, and in over-
population.

739 "Sharing the hardest decision," by W. M.
Gaylin. HOSPITAL PHYSICIAN. 8:33, passim,
July, 1972.
The decision as to whether or not a
seemingly terminally ill patient should
live or die is a most difficult one.
Many sources should be brought to bear

on the situation, and the interaction of many individuals is essential. The author seeks to explain who should share in the euthanasia decision and why.

740 "Should Americans have the right to die with dignity," THE NATIONAL OBSERVER. 3/4-1, 1972.

741 "Should we prolong suffering," by E. Davis. NEBRASKA STATE MEDICAL JOURNAL. 35(10):310-312, October, 1950.
 Discusses the tremendous strides medical science has made and discusses the growing number of older individuals living in today's society. Considers forms of passive euthanasia.

742 "Soliloquy on death," by A. Feigenbaum. HOSPITAL MANAGEMENT. 97:11, June, 1964.

743 "Soliloquy on death," by T. Hale. HOSPITAL MANAGEMENT. 97:11, passim, April, 1964.

744 "Soliloquy on death," by C. W. Letourneau. HOSPITAL MANAGEMENT. 96:58, passim, November, 1963.

745 "Some overtones of euthanasia," by E. E. Filbey. HOSPITAL TOPICS. 43:55-58, passim, September, 1965.

746 "The spirit: who will make the choice of life and death?" TIME. 97:48, passim, April 19, 1971.
 The new genetics poses a serious threat to the sanctity of life and the solidarity of the family as an institution. Experiments in human cloning or xeroxing, artificial insemination and doner mothers are developing faster than the wisdom to manage them. Scientific advances can promote human freedom or inhibit it, but the writer asserts the distinctions are

not always obvious.

747 "Still euthanasia," by W. R. Brandli.
     CHRISTIAN CENTURY. 84:471, April 12, 1967,
        Presented is a letter supporting M. M.
     Shideler stand concerning euthanasia.
     (CHRISTIAN CENTURY. 83:1499-1502, December
     7, 1966).

748 "Struggle for the right to automathanasia
     in cases of autoeuthanasia," by A.
     Wonza. POLSKI TYGOONIK LEKARSKI. (Was-
     szawa) 26:1994-1996, December 20, 1971.
     (Polish)

749 "Survie purement vegetative dans la cere-
     brosclerose; euthanasie, dysthanasie,
     orthothanasie (Purely vegetative survival
     in cerebrosclerosis; euthanasia, dysthanasia
     and orthothanasia," by J. Roskam. REVUE
     MEDICALE DE LIEGE. 5(20):709-713, October
     19, 1950.

750 "Symposium on death. and attitudes toward
     death," GERIATRICS. 27:52, passim,
     August, 1972.
        A symposium was held to discuss death;
     that which should be told the patient and
     the current status of euthanasia. Views
     of nine participants are presented.

751 "Symposium on euthanasia - introduction,"
     MARYLAND STATE MEDICAL JOURNAL. 2(3):120,
     March, 1963.
        Introduces the articles presented in
     this report. These articles are: "Legal
     aspects relating to euthanasia," by C. E.
     Ortho, Jr; "Medical aspects relating to
     euthanasia," by L. Krause; "The sanctity
     of life," by G. Boas; and "Question and
     answer period".

752 "Symposium on euthanasia - question and
     answer period," MARYLAND STATE MEDICAL
     JOURNAL. 2(3):136-140, March, 1953.

The participants questioned the assertions made in the papers presented at the symposium.

753 "Tact facing life and death," by E. L. Keyes. THE PROCEEDINGS OF THE CHARAKA CLUB. 10:45-48, 1941.

754 "Technologic progress and the Hippocratic Oath," by C. Berkley. AMERICAN JOURNAL OF MEDICAL ELECTRONICS. 3:1-2, January-March, 1964.

755 "Thanatopsis revisited - editorial," JOURNAL OF THE KANSAS MEDICAL SOCIETY. 73:305-329, June, 1972.
With the implementation of euthanasia, medical science needs aid in establishing a system of checks and balances to control its administration.

756 "There is no difference between outright euthanasia and the withdrawing of treatment when death is certain says Professor Louis C. Lasagna." THE NATIONAL OBSERVER. 4/28-13, 1973.

757 "These are the hard questions: What is death? Who shall say? Who shall live? How long?," by G. W. Downey. MODERN NURSING HOME. 29:72-74, September, 1972.
Death with dignity is a right inherent to all individuals, Downey asserts. Additionally, he structures a comparison and contrast essay as he gives answers to the questions proposed in the title of this article.

758 "They shall live," by W. J. Marx. AMERICAN SCHOLAR. 8(2):253-255, April, 1939.
Lennox's article, "Should they live?" is discussed as Marx attempts to find flaws in Lennox's argument. (see: AMERICAN SCHOLAR. 7:454-456, October, 1938)

759 "This I believe...about questioning the
     right to die," by M. W. Shepard. NURSING
     OUTLOOK. 16:22-25, October, 1968.
        Feels that a society that uses its tech-
     nology to promote longevity for its members,
     yet rejects these members when they are
     no longer self-sufficient, commits a grave
     injustice. Shepard examines the reasons
     behind the prolonging of life and also the
     consideration for ending it. She suggests
     that everyone develop a personal philoso-
     phy regarding dying and death, and that one
     be allowed the freedom to die if one's
     suffering is being prolonged.

760 "Three score years and twelve?" CHRISTIANITY
     TODAY. 17:36, February 16, 1973.
     By pointing out the inconsistency and irra-
     tionality of a group in Chautauqua County,
     New York, the writer discredits the pro-
     posal of that group which agrees to sui-
     cide at age 72 and mandatory death at age
     144.

761 "Treating incurables," SCIENCE NEWSLETTER.
     80:300, November 4, 1961.
     The doctor's job is to keep the patient
     alive as long as he can, asserts this edi-
     torialist. Treating the incurable is a
     legal responsibility as well as a medical
     one, states Dr. David A. Karnofsky.

762 "Triology in four voices," by C. Koupernik.
     CONCOURS MEDICAL. 85:2155-2156, April
     6, 1963. (French)

763 "Vegetables," by R. Lamerton. NURSING
     TIMES. 70:1180-1185, August 1, 1974.
        States that terminology can often close
     one's vision of a situation. The word
     "vegetable" for example, may hinder one's
     willingness to give assistance.

GENERAL PERIODICAL LITERATURE

764 "Voluntary death," SPECTATOR. 184:599, May 5, 1950.

765 "Voluntary euthanasia," LANCET. 2(24): 775, December 9, 1950.

766 "Voluntary euthanasia," by John Lister.
NEW ENGLAND JOURNAL OF MEDICINE. 280
(22):1225-1227, May 20, 1969.
Discusses the topic of euthanasia first from the legal and then from the moral viewpoint. The author relies heavily on articles appearing in SPECTATOR (March 28, 1969), THE OBSERVER (March 30, 1969), THE TIMES (March 24, 1969) and NEW ENGLAND JOURNAL OF MEDICINE (239: 985-990, 1948).

767 "Voluntary mercy deaths: sociological aspects of euthanasia," by Arthur A. Levisohn. JOURNAL OF FORENSIC MEDICINE. 8(2):59-79, April-June, 1969.
Multiple legal, medical and moral views are discussed.

768 "What recourse for the hopelessly ill?" by M. M. Shideler. CHRISTIAN CENTURY. 84:272-273, March 1, 1967.
In response , Mrs. Shideler refutes criticisms of her "Coup de Grace" article (CHRISTIAN CENTURY. 83:1499-1502), made by Mr. Hackmose, Mr. Moffett and Mr. Wilson.

769 "When do we have the right to die: three case histories," by P. Wilkes. LIFE. 72:48-52, January 14, 1972.

770 "When is life out of the physician's hands?" AMERICAN MEDICAL NEWS. 16:8-10, January 15, 1973.

771 "When life is no longer life," by M.
Fishbein. MEDICAL WORLD NEWS. 15:84,
March 15, 1974.
Euthanasia raises medical, legal, and
moral questions that have been endlessly
debated by members of all professions
concerned with the individual and his
welfare. Cases are reviewed and statistics
concerning 250 Chicago internists and
surgeons opinions are supplied.

772 "When should a patient be allowed to die -
editorial," by Herrick Peterson.
HOSPITAL PHYSICIAN. 8:15, July, 1972.
Attempts to persuade moralists and
lawmakers to help answer the title-
question - when should a patient be
allowed to die.

NEWSPAPER ARTICLES

773 "A. Shaw article maintains that parents
of mongoloids with potentially deadly
but surgically correctable defects have
legal and moral responsibility to determine if child should live or die,"
NEW YORK TIMES. IV. 44, January 30,
1972.

774 "Alienist recommends committal of
mercy killer to asylum," NEW YORK
TIMES. 27:2, July 22, 1930.

775 "American Academy of General Practice
heads seek to keep issue from conference -
St. Louis," NEW YORK TIMES. 4:7,
February 21, 1950.

776 "Backing by a number of Chicago physicians-
Dr. Haiselden's editorial on euthanasia,"
NEW YORK TIMES. 4:3, November 16, 1917.

777 "Comment," NEW YORK TIMES. II. 10:6,
February 19, 1939 and IV. 2:1, February 19,
1939.

778 "Dr. J. C. White holds lobotomy as legal
substitute," NEW YORK TIMES. 37:3,
October 27, 1950.

779 "Dr. J. H. Pincus, Jr. letter discusses
severe dangers involved in euthanasia,"
NEW YORK TIMES. 40:3, January 24, 1973.

780 "Editorial - prolonging death," WASHINGTON
POST. Section a, 14:4, May 18, 1968.

781 "Ernest Morgan on David Dempsey's June 23
article on the 'Living Will' ; describes
his mother's decision to die," NEW YORK
TIMES. VI. p. 14, September 29, 1974.

782 "Euthanasia - feature article; illus," NEW
YORK TIMES. VIII. 5:1, October 22
1933.

783 "Euthanasia Society president Reverend
C. F. Potter says mercy killing is widespread among doctors," NEW YORK TIMES.
42:3, January 9, 1950.

784 "Fined $50.00 for confessed plot to kill
aunt to relieve her suffering, Cincinatti,
Ohio," NEW YORK TIMES. II. 5:2, March
31, 1935.

785 "First degree murder charge to be pressed,"
NEW YORK TIMES. 8:2, January 15, 1939.

786 "Grand jury refuses to indict father, J,
for mercy killing," NEW YORK TIMES. 34:
4, January 16, 1932.

787 "Group of doctors, testifying at hearings
on death.with dignity ... disagree on
whether terminally ill or injured patients
have right to euthanasia," NEW YORK TIMES.
15:1, August 8, 1972.

788 "Hospital scouts claim," NEW YORK TIMES.
26:5, February 24, 1954.

789 "J. Bevan article on euthanasia debate -
G. B.," NEW YORK TIMES. VI. p. 14,
August 9, 1959.

790 "Killed by father, A., as an act of mercy,"
NEW YORK TIMES. 19:4, July 13, 1930.

791 "Killed by foster son, who claims killing
was act of mercy; his attempt at suicide
fails," NEW YORK TIMES. 3:5, December 16,
1932.

792 "Killed by wife in mercy killing," NEW
YORK TIMES. 34:2, April 25, 1932.

793 "Letter by Dr. Kennedy," NEW YORK TIMES.
20:7, February 22, 1939.

794 "Letter urging legal status," NEW YORK
TIMES. 20:6, May 19, 1939.

795 "Letters," NEW YORK TIMES. VI. 4:4,5,
August 23, 1959.

796 "Letters by Dr. B. Sachs," NEW YORK TIMES.
16:7, February 20, 1939 and 18:7, February
21, 1939.

797 "Letters on Dr. A. Shaw, January 30 article
on mongolism, Shaw comments," NEW YORK
TIMES. VI. p. 22, February 27, 1972.

798 "Letter by Nixdorff," NEW YORK TIMES.
12:7, January 30, 1939.

799 "Lunacy committee to test mercy killer
of his sanity," NEW YORK TIMES. 3:3,
July 14, 1930.

800 "Mass. Medical Society denies euthanasia is
common among doctors," NEW YORK TIMES.

15:4, January 10, 1950.

801 "Mercy killer is sent to Binghamton State Hospital," NEW YORK TIMES. 22:1, July 23, 1930.

802 "Mercy killing investigation," NEW YORK TIMES. 34:3, October 3, 1938.

803 "Mother kills him and self to end his suffering," NEW YORK TIMES. 7:4, June 4, 1934.

804 "Mrs. J. Berler, D. Strecker and G. P. Selth letters commenting on E. Freeman's May 21 article on mercy deaths involving victims of open spine disorder," NEW YORK TIMES. VI. p. 34, June 11, 1972.

805 "NBC close-up series to broadcast "The right to die" on ability of medical science to sustain human life in face of death," NEW YORK TIMES. 61:1, January 4, 1974.

806 "N. J. alienists find Sell was insane during slaying," NEW YORK TIMES. 56:6, April 2, 1953.

807 "NEW YORK TIMES survey of changing attitudes toward death; says Americans are increasingly trying to come to grips with and ease inevitability of their mortality; demand is growing for right to die and death with dignity," NEW YORK TIMES. 1:6, July 21, 1974.

808 "NYU Medical School freshman orientation meeting on current medical problems discusses euthanasia," NEW YORK TIMES. 40:1, September 10, 1972.

809 "On euthanasia - editorial," NEW YORK TIMES. 8:4, May 18, 1914.

810 "Pleads not guilty to charge of murder for dashing seriously injured daughter to rocks; pleads mercy act," NEW YORK TIMES. 15:3, August 29, 1933.

811 "Police find no evidence to substantiate story," NEW YORK TIMES. 5:8, November 22, 1935 and IV. 9:5, November 24, 1935.

812 "Russian seaman with terminal cancer enroute to U. S. for flight back to USSR dies," NEW YORK TIMES. 35:7, January 24, 1972.

813 "Ruth P. Mack letter on Dr. Frederic Greenberg's April 22 article," NEW YORK TIMES. 30:4, May 18, 1974.

814 "Special article by W. G. Tinckon-Fernandez on putting to death incurable diseased persons," NEW YORK TIMES. IX. 9:1, March 22, 1925.

815 "Two experts named," NEW YORK TIMES. 3:6, July 17, 1930.

816 "Two sisters released from insane asylum after serving sentence for slaying imbecile brother in 1935," NEW YORK TIMES. 7:4, September 23, 1936.

817 "U.S.C. helicopter carries stricken crewmen from Polish fishing vessel 15.5 miles off N. J. to Atlantic City Hospital after he apparently suffered a heart attack," NEW YORK TIMES. 14:3, January 28, 1972.

818 "Urged by Quisling Government official for hopelessly insane, Norway," NEW YORK TIMES. 3:7, August 17, 1942.

819 "Who is incurable? a query and reply," NEW YORK TIMES. Section 8. 5:1, October 22, 1933.

820 "Article," by P. H. Muller. WORLD MEDICAL
     JOURNAL. September-October, 1967.
       States that there are times when the
     doctor must assume responsibility in
     terminating a seemingly useless struggle.

821 "Britons would alter decalogue to end
     incurable pain," NEWSWEEK. 6:40,
     November 16, 1935.

822 "Case for euthanasia," by C. K. Millard.
     FORTNIGHTLY REVIEW. 136:701-718,
     December, 1931.

823 "Case for voluntary euthanasia," by E.
     Slater. CONTEMPORARY REVIEW. 219:84-
     88, August, 1971.
       Every individual should have the right
     to chose between living and dying.
     Consideration is given to the human right,
     medical ethics, old age, and the act of
     dying. Emphasis is placed on who has a
     right to die, when one should chose death,
     and who is ultimately responsible for
     an individual's death.

824 "A defense of mercy killing," by Ingemar
     Hedenius. ATLAS. 7:229-231, April,
     1964.

825 "Doctor who chose death for his patients,"
     NEWSWEEK. 50:54, July 8, 1957.
       One should not kill, but one should
     not strive to officiously keep alive,
     comments Dr. Stewart Noy Scott on his
     practices of active and passive eutha-
     nasia during his medical career.

826 "Editorial: death and dying," by R. F.
     Newcomb. RN. 35:1, August, 1972.
       Informs readers about the Good Death
     Fellowship and its quarterly publication
     of Euthanasia News. This fellowship
     states that its purpose is to help people

achieve a good death without pain, in
dignity and peace.

827 "Ethics and euthanasia," by J. Fletcher.
AMERICAN JOURNAL OF NURSING. 73:670-
675, April, 1973.
    Joseph Fletcher presents a moral defense
for positive euthanasia by incorporating
humanization into the dying process.

828 "Euthanasia," by S. D. Williams. FORT-
NIGHTLY REVIEW., 1872.
    Argues in support of a voluntary eutha-
nasia plan.

829 "Euthanasia at 80? proposal by British
Health Officer," NEWSWEEK. 73:77, May
12, 1969.

830 "The Euthanasia Educational Fund limits
itself to promoting passive euthanasia
among doctors," THE NATIONAL OBSERVER.
3/4-1, 1972.

831 "Euthanasia is an act of love," by P.
Torrissi. SEVENTEEN. 33:116, August,
1974.
    Believes that when the practice of
keeping dying patient alive contributes
to the prolonged suffering and overwhelming emotional and financial burdens
on the family, the saving of that life
can no longer be considered a gain.
"Living Will" is also discussed.

832 "Euthanasia, pro and con, a human necessity,"
by H. Benjamin. NATION. 170:79-80,
January 28, 1950.
    Asserts that those critics who claim
that euthanasia is immoral on the grounds
that what is hopelessly ill today may be
curable tomorrow are mistaken. Proposed
or projected cures are ineffectual for
the hopeless cancer victim or the imbecile

child. Pro-euthanasia arguments are
presented by refutation arguments against
it. A case history of a family's financial
problems is presented as grounds for
further euthanasia legislation.

833 "Euthanasia, right or wrong," by S. James.
     SURVEY GRAPHIC. 37:241-243, May, 1948.
        Is active euthanasia right or wrong?
     Presents facts in defense of active eutha-
     nasia as a means to end the suffering of
     terminal patients.

834 "Give man the right to die, British MD
     says," JOURNAL OF THE AMERICAN MEDICAL
     ASSOCIATION. 210:657, October 27, 1969.
        A British physician, Dr. Slater, argues
     in support of a voluntary euthanasia
     plan. He insists that the choice of death
     may be a reasonably rational choice under
     extreme conditions.

835 "Legalized suicide," by William T. Hall.
     DELAWARE STATE MEDICAL JOURNAL. 40:50-
     51, February, 1968.
        Dr. Hall has discussed the act of dying
     with elderly members of his own family
     and with many of his dying patients.
     He concludes that they would vote ten to
     one in favor of legalized suicide.

836 "Letter," by H. S. Blatch. FORUM. 94:323,
     December, 1935.
        Supports the theory of the individual's
     inherent right to end his own life.
     Empetus for this letter was C. P. Gilman's
     "Right to die" article. (FORUM. 94:
     297-300, 1935.)

837 "Letter to the editor," by C. C. Catt.
     FORUM. 94:324, December, 1935.
        Mrs. Gilman's suicide and her article
     find support. See also: FORUM. 94:
     297-300, 1935.

838 "Liege trial and the problem of voluntary
euthanasia," by L. Colebrook. LANCET.
2:1225-1226, December 8, 1962. Also:
editorial, p. 1205.
"The Euthanasia Society believes the
time has come for a serious reappraisal
of the advantages and difficulties and
possible dangers that might result from
the legalization of voluntary euthanasia.
In a recent publication, "A Plan for
Voluntary Euthanasia," the society put
forward proposals that it commends to
both layman and medical staff," (p. 1225)

839 "Limitation of life, editorial," NORTHWEST
MEDICINE. 69:487, July, 1970.
The editor asks, "Is it time to abandon
the principle handed down by Hippocrates?"
Williams presents powerful arguments for
acceptance of euthanasia. A forum for
and against the proposals made by Williams
is provided in the correspondence section
of this issue.

840 "The limits of euthanasia," by L. A.
Tollemache. THE SPECTATOR. 46:240,
1873.
A letter to the editor is presented
in which Mr. Tollemache explains his
position on voluntary euthanasia. He
advocates the "summary extinction of
idiots and persons in their dotage".

841 "Mercy death for incurables should be made
legal," DAILY COMPASS. page 8, August
24, 1949.
Argues in favor of a voluntary euthanasia plan.

842 "Mercy killing advocates of America and
Brittain form organization," NEWSWEEK.
11:26, January 31, 1938.
Seeing a loved one die a lingering
death with a painful illness is alarming.

Suggests in such instances euthanasia may appear a reasonable alternative. Cases are sited as well as legislation briefly discussed.

843 "Murder by request," by A. M. Turano. AMERICAN MERCURY. 36:423-429, December, 1935.
Mercy toward a suffering animal is a commonly accepted practice. In fact, it is often mandatory, and the individual refusing to put to a merciful end a suffering animal may be fined or imprisoned. Yet, if a human being were to do the same for another human being, he is condemned and called a murderer. Oftentimes, the individual who performs a euthanasia act, takes his own life. Monstrosities and hopelessly injured individuals are left to live on useless lives. The entire idea of life and dying; suffering and pain; the act of dying and of prolonging dying need to be reevaluated and the conclusion reached that society cannot logically deny afflicted citizens of their individual right to chose to die.

844 "The new cure for incurables," by L. A. Tollemache. FORTNIGHTLY REVIEW. 19:218, passim, 1873.
Argues in support of a voluntary euthanasia plan and offers a plan for the elimination of incurables.

845 "New support for doctor - aided deaths," by J. Carlova. MEDICAL ECONOMICS. 47: 254-258, May 25, 1970.

846 "Number, types and duration of human lives," by R. H. Williams. NORTHWEST MEDICINE. 69:493-496, July, 1970.
Planning to prevent over-population, by definition, must encompass the practice

of all forms of euthanasia. Euthanasia should be considered a form of treatment to be offered to the severely ill (mental or physical). In many instances, death can be a welcomed alternative to a life of prolonged suffering.

847 "Officiously to keep alive?" by A. Brass. JOURNAL OF THE AMERICAN MEDICAL ASSOCIATION. 214:905-907, November 2, 1970.
A. Brass discusses cases where euthanasia might be considered. Opinion polls are quoted along with an analysis of areas where euthanasia legislation seems necessary.

848 "Permission to die," by E. J. Cassell. BIOSCIENCE. 23:475-478, August, 1973.
Two problems stand out around which the problem of euthanasia crystallizes: the definition of man as a person, and the dimension of trust. "In the case of the dying or the aged, based in trust, and in the service of the good death, the physician can give permission for the person to stop the battle of life. He can give permission to die," p. 477

849 "Pleasures of dying," by E. P. Buffet. NEW ENGLANDER AND YALE REVIEW. 55:231-242, September, 1891.
Discusses the origins of the development of the belief that death as an event is intrinsically painful. Suggests by inference that many deaths are not painful, and only the events leading to death are painful. Concludes that euthanasia, as the happy death, is to be desired by all.

850 "The principle of euthanasia," by G. N. Anthony. PLAIN VIEW. 11:188-204, November, 1957.
Favors establishing a legal right to

the practice of euthanasia.

851 "Right and wrong of mercy killing; symposium -
     it is right to grant easy death," LITERARY
     DIGEST. 124(Digest):22, October 23, 1937.
        Nine articles are presented in support
     of specific forms of euthanasia. Aspects
     of euthanasia employment to relieve pain,
     accelerate the process of dying in a
     terminal illness and capital punishment
     are analyzed. Reviews ideas supporting
     a euthanasia plan.

852 "Right to die," LANCET. 2:926, October 31,
     1970.
        Calls upon doctors to begin alleviating
     suffering instead of prolonging a human
     existence, which can never again be
     restored to its original quality.

853 "Right to die," by Joseph Fletcher.
     ATLANTIC. 221:62-64, April, 1968.
        Argues for active "honest" euthanasia.
     Sites the case of Mr. & Mrs. Bernard Bard
     and their mongoloid son, Philip and
     supports the Bard's views concerning the
     subject of euthanasia. Argues theo-
     logically and presents a strong case for
     the legalization of voluntary euthanasia.

854 "Right to die," by C. P. Gilman. FORUM.
     94:297-300, November, 1935.
        A plea by Mrs. Gilman for a more
     enlightened attitude toward euthanasia
     and suicide. The article was pub-
     lished after Mrs. Gilman's suicide in
     August, 1935.

855 "Right to die," by S. L. Henderson Smith.
     LANCET. 2:1088-1089, November 21, 1970.
        Proports a new philosophical approach
     to death whereby death might be chosen as
     a reasonable rational solution to the pro-
     blem of a terminal or severe illness.

856 "Right to die," by M. Mead. NURSING
OUTLOOK. 16:20-21, October, 1968.
In Margaret Mead's opinion, we should
have the right not to be saved when
medical intervention would restore organ
function but not restore the patient to
a sentient human being again. She
believes that while in sound mind, one
should make a legal statement concerning
one's wishes regarding the prolongation
of life under irremediable conditions.
Once made, the old or terminally ill
can live out the remainder of their lives
without the haunting fear of witless
dependency.

857 "Right to die - a debate," by A. L. Wolbarst.
FORUM. 94:330-334, December, 1935.
Covers various aspects of the legal
questions which arise when euthanasia
is considered. The article presents a
discussion about euthanasia in relation
to the incurably ill, the imbecile, and
the insane.

858 "Right to die - a father speaks," by B.
Bard, et al. ATLANTIC MONTHLY. 221:
59-62, April, 1968.
Mr. Bard argues for the right of the
hopelessly mongoloid infant to die. He
cites the case of his son and describes
the events which surrounded his, his wife's
and his son's very short existence. Mr.
Bard implies support for a form of euthanasia in these cases and he suggests that
the whole subject of euthanasia needs
to be reexamined.

859 "Right to die in peace: mentally competent
adult in Florida may refuse further life-
sustaining treatment," NEWSLETTER.
(SOCIETY OF HOSPITAL ATTORNEYS). 4:1,
August, 1971. (Pt. 1)

860 "The right to die - II - dinner in Thessaly,"
by Sherwood Anderson. FORUM. 95:40-41,
January 1936.
Comes to the defense and praise of
Charlotte Gilman's suicide. Talks about
the "good life" not merely life and
discusses man's inherent right to end
his own life if he so chooses.

861 "The right to kill," TIME. 26:53, passim,
November 18, 1935.
An anonymous physician wrote a letter
to the London Daily Mail concerning five
medical situations which led him to
commit mercy killing. The subsequent
responses from scientists, doctors, and
legislators are presented.

862 "The right to kill - continued," TIME.
26:37-38, passim, December 2, 1935.
Discusses the physician's right to
perform euthanasias on defective newborns and suffering incurables. Case
histories provide additional supportive
information.

863 "Should mercy killing be permitted. Dr.
Leslie Wenger says yes, with GOOD
HOUSEKEEPING poll," GOOD HOUSEKEEPING.
164:82, April, 1967.

864 "Should they live? Certain economic aspects
of medicine; number of unproductive members
which society can support is limited,"
by W. G. Lennox. AMERICAN SCHOLAR. 7(4):
454-456, October, 1938.
Lennox advocates the quiet, painless
euthanizing of defectives of the lowest
type as well as the sterilization of
others and the spreading of contraceptive
information to the lower classes.

865 "Swedish health board sanctions euthanasia
by MD," MEDICAL WORLD NEWS. 5:56-57, 60,
November 20, 1964.

GENERAL: FOR EUTHANASIA

A limited form of dodschjälp - death help - has been sanctioned by the Swedish National Board of Health. The specifics of the "death help" situation are defined as well as counter-opposing views presented including Dr. Alexander's analogy of World War II mass murders in Germany.

866 "To be or not to be: voluntary euthanasia bill," NURSING TIMES. 65:382, March 20, 1969.
The purpose of the Voluntary Euthanasia Bill is to authorize physicians to practice euthanasia on patients with irremediable conditions, providing that the patient has signed a declaration requesting euthanasia not less than 30 days before enactment. The eight clauses that must be signed by the patient requesting euthanasia are discussed briefly.

NEWSPAPER ARTICLES

867 "American Association of Progressive Medicine--annual convention; suggestion of Dr. W. A. Guild for legalized euthanasia providing death for hopeless invalids receives support of majority of delegates," NEW YORK TIMES. September 25, 8:2, 1917.

868 "American Euthanasia Society hails Universal International Pictures for motion picture 'An Act of Mercy'," NEW YORK TIMES. 33: 2, January 12, 1949.

869 "Anonymous letter on David Dempsey's June 23 article on the living will and right to euthanasia and death with dignity; suggests right to suicide be made use of by terminally ill patients; relates incident of his wife's suicide after her bout with cancer," NEW YORK TIMES. VI. p. 29, July 7, 1974.

GENERAL: FOR EUTHANASIA

870 "British Dr. Dobbs reports mothers ask her
     for drugs to kill families painlessly in
     event of nuclear war," NEW YORK TIMES.
     48:8, December, 1961.

871 "British physician admits five killings;
     Lord Moynihan starts campaign to give
     incurables the right to die; Drs. H. Cou-
     tard and M. Cutler and I. Goldston condemn
     killings," NEW YORK TIMES. 1:5, November
     8, 1935.

872 "Britons debate issue after Dr. Millard re-
     ports giving cancer victim sleep-inducing
     drugs until she died," NEW YORK TIMES.
     49:1, May 6, 1959.

873 "Canon Lowe approves it for all over 70,
     G. B. as population curb," NEW YORK TIMES.
     12:6, November 25, 1952.

874 "Defended by Dr. O. Riddle, Dr. F. Kennedy
     and Dr. C. E. Nixdorff," NEW YORK TIMES.
     2:6, February 14, 1939.

875 "Dr. E. A. Barton admits taking life of in-
     curable patient; urges sufferers right to
     die, Voluntary Euthanasia Legalization
     Society, London," NEW YORK TIMES. 21:6,
     May 22, 1947.

876 "Dr. G. L. Carlisle says extreme measures
     are justified when death seems inevitable
     for patient," NEW YORK TIMES. 29:7,
     November 6, 1935.

877 "Dr. C. E. Farr opposed but would not act
     to prolong life if it brings suffering,"
     NEW YORK TIMES. 21:8, January 28, 1936.

878 "Dr. A. L. Goldwater says many doctors en-
     able incurable patients to die by providing
     them with overdoses of morphine," NEW
     YORK TIMES. 33:5, 22, January 18, 1950.

GENERAL: FOR EUTHANASIA

879 "Dr. V. Hampton named president elect; Dr.
    R. P. Morhardt holds lives of incurables
    should not be prolonged," NEW YORK TIMES.
    11:4, July 20, 1951.

880 "Dr. A. Lorenz views them as justified under
    proper circumstances," NEW YORK TIMES.
    56:4, November 28, 1935.

881 "Dr. W. R. Malthews, dean of St. Pauls, Lon-
    don, backs euthanasia," NEW YORK TIMES.
    7:4, May 3, 1950.

882 "Dr. I. C. Philbrick supports euthanasia
    measure on radio; medical group opposed,"
    NEW YORK TIMES. 17:1, February 14, 1937.

883 "Dr. M. A. Warriner favors killing of in-
    curable patients; confesses to killing
    A. LeTourneau," NEW YORK TIMES. 25:6,
    Novmeber 20, 1935.

884 "Dr. Weatherall defends euthanasia," NEW
    YORK TIMES. 16:3, May 7, 1959.

885 "Dr. Weatherhead defends euthanasia," NEW
    YORK TIMES. 16:3, May 7, 1959.

886 "Euthanasia Society of America to seek in
    NH 1st mercy death law permitting volun-
    tary euthanasia," NEW YORK TIMES. 7:1,
    January 3, 1950.

887 "GB... royal committee to study W. L. Ding-
    ley view urging euthanasia for defective
    infants," NEW YORK TIMES. 43:1, Febru-
    ary 20, 1955.

888 "Gallup poll shows 46% for it in US, 69%
    in Great Britain," NEW YORK TIMES. III.
    4:1, April 23, 1939.

889 "Growing number of U.S. proponents of eutha-
    nasia discussed," NEW YORK TIMES. March 1,
    1971.

138

GENERAL: FOR EUTHANASIA

890 "H. M. Kallen holds voluntary euthanasia in-
     alienable right," NEW YORK TIMES. 3:6,
     June 21, 1958.

891 "Illinois Medical Association asks painless
     death sleep for incurable," NEW YORK TIMES.
     4:3, May 9, 1931.

892 "Letter from doctor backs legal euthanasia
     with proper safeguards of medical panel
     and request by patient for end to suffer-
     ing," NEW YORK TIMES. 24:6, February 20,
     1950.

893 "Mercy death for incurables should be made
     legal," by Gertrude Anne Edwards. DAILY
     COMPASS. p. 8, August 28, 1949.
        Claims 3,272 physicians favored volun-
     tary euthanasia as a result of an inquiry
     which the writer made.

894 "Montreal Alderman would destroy woman drug
     addict," NEW YORK TIMES. II. 2:4, Sept-
     ember 9, 1934.

895 "NYS Medical Society adopts resolution affir-
     ming patients right to die with dignity
     when there is irrefutable evidence that
     biological death is inevitable," NEW YORK
     TIMES. 35:2, January 13, 1973.

896 "NYS Medical Society opposes euthanasia,"
     NEW YORK TIMES. 29:1, May 10, 1950.

897 "O. R. Russell article holds that each per-
     son has right to die in dignity but is
     denied that right under law that forbids
     him to direct what happens to him personally
     in event he is stricken with painful in-
     curable illness," NEW YORK TIMES. 29:4,
     February 14, 1972.

898 "Retired doctor admits committing mercy
     killings," THE GREENVILLE NEWS. November

7, 1974.
A British surgeon says he has conducted mercy killings on patients throughout his medical career.

899 "S. F. Baldwin letter supports Prs. Nixon in his statement that certain crimes demand death penalty, but does not support carrying out such a sentence by traditional means and calls for practice of euthanasia," NEW YORK TIMES. 42:4, March 22, 1973.

900 "Survey by Medical Opinion magazine finds acceptance of euthanasia has become widespread in the medical profession; finds that on choosing how to die, 79% of the doctors agree totally or in some circumstances that people have the right to make their wishes known before serious illness strikes; and on terminal care, 82% would practice forms of passive euthanasia on members of families; 86% on themselves," NEW YORK TIMES. IV. 7:2, June 16, 1974.

GENERAL: AGAINST EUTHANASIA

901 "Against euthanasia," LANCET. 1:220, January 30, 1971.
A panel appointed by the Board of Science and Education of the British Medical Association has voted strongly against euthanasia. In the report, the panel suggests that what is needed is not euthanasia legislation but more resourceful treatment for the chronically ill and a change of attitude toward these patients.

902 "The American Medical Association approved a guideline saying physicians need not use extraordinary means to prolong life when there is irrefutable evidence that death is imminent," THE NATIONAL OBSERVER.

GENERAL: AGAINST EUTHANASIA

12/15-5, 1973.

903 "Case against mercy killing," by W. L.
Sperry. AMERICAN MERCURY. 70:271-278,
March, 1950.

904 "Comments against euthanasia," by C. S.
Frischkorn. JOURNAL OF THE NATIONAL
MEDICAL SOCIETY. 4(3-4):83, July-December, 1948.

905 "Euthanasia," JOURNAL OF THE MISSISSIPPI
STATE MEDICAL ASSOCIATION. 2:184-185,
April, 1961.
The alarming popularity of active
euthanasia and its new-found impetus
among medical and more non-medical
personnel is in direct conflict with the
physician's commitment to preserve life.
The doctor feels that euthanasia has
such a catabolic effect that it should
never be advocated by someone in the
medical field.

906 "Euthanasia," by R. Lamerton. NURSING
TIMES. 70:260, February 21, 1974.
Lamerton asserts that it is not the
question of euthanasia being right or
wrong, desirable or repugnant, but rather
that it is just irrelevant. He claims
that once the pain, anxiety, nausea, etc.,
are pushed into the background, the
desire for euthanasia vaporizes.

907 "Euthanasia," by F. Rud. JOURNAL OF
CLINICAL AND EXPERIMENTAL PSYCHOPATHOLOGY.
14(1):1-12, March, 1953.
In this article is provided an analysis
of the problem of euthanasia from the
viewpoints of legal philosophy, natural
science, religion, and medical jurisprudence. The author attempts to show-up
many of the paralogisms used in attacking
and defending euthanasia. Dr. Rud

concludes that euthanasia is not a right
of man, and that he regrets it as a
method of relief.

908 "Euthanasia and murder," by G. K. Chesterton. AMERICAN REVIEW. 8:487-490, February, 1937.
    Suggests that laws are created to
prevent one from doing "things" he would
like or enjoy doing. Chesterton structures
an argument against euthanasia by comparison. Since we all have a bit of the
criminal within ourselves, Chesterton
claims, we must structure laws to prevent us from acting foolishly.

909 "Euthanasia as a violation of the principles of humanity," by G. Herold.
MEDIZINISCHE KLINIK (Munchen). 55:1446-
1447, August 12, 1960. (German)

910 "Euthanasia, capital punishment, murder,"
by A. T. W. Simeons. INDIAN MEDICAL
GAZETTE. 83:327-329, July, 1948.
    Claims that no one really wishes to die.
Euthanasia, whether human or animal, does
not put the patient or animal out of his
misery, but rather removes the suffering
and sufferer from our sight. The sugges-
is made that this is not mercy.

911 "Euthanasia from the physician's point of
view," AMERICAN MONTHLY: REVIEW OF
REVIEWS. 33:628-629, May, 1906.
    In VRAGEN VAN DEN DAG (1906) Dr. H.
Pinkhof formulates his views as to the
physician's duty concerning the theory
of euthanasia. The physician, Pinkhof
suggests, must follow his traditional
duty to save, preserve, and prolong life.
Suffering and pain are to be relieved,
and the sufferer can produce good by the
example of his courage.

912   "Euthanasia; medical opinion," by A. M.
      Schwitalla. LINACRE QUARTERLY. 14(2):
      16-26, April, 1947.
         Opposes use of euthanasia in medical
      practice ... and explains the extent of
      powers a doctor has when treating his
      patients.

913   "Euthanasia rejected by French Academy of
      Moral and Political Sciences." TODAY'S
      HEALTH. 28:65, April, 1950.
         The French Academy of Moral and Poli-
      tical Sciences has made a bold rejection
      of any form of euthanasia. Highlighted
      in the article is a recount of recent
      experiences involving the Nazi's death
      chamber.

914   "Euthanasia: to be or not to be," by F.
      Kennedy. COLLIER'S. 125:13, 48-51,
      April 22, 1950.
         From a presentation of case histories,
      Dr. Kennedy argues that one can never
      infallibly know when an illness is incur-
      able. In the article, Dr. Kennedy states
      his opposition to the idea of euthanasia
      and the reasons for his opinions.

915   "A false mercy," by Martin Gumpert.
      NATION. 170:80, January 28, 1950.
         Claims that the act of euthanasia is
      a form of false mercy, and that too great
      a responsibility which burdens the physi-
      cian exists. Additionally, he argues that
      the concept of euthanasia being the good
      death is out of date with the current
      study of modern medicine.

916   "Former National Cancer Institute official
      against euthanasia," by R. W. Rhein.
      U. S. MEDICINE. 8:1, passim, August 15,
      1972.

917 "God squad: life should be safeguarded,"
     by Joseph L. Lennon. RHODE ISLAND MED-
     ICAL JOURNAL. 57:334-337, August, 1974.
     Discusses the medical dilemmas which
     society must currently face, such as the
     prolongation of the lives of retarded
     and infants with birth defects, and the
     length of time which a dying patient's
     life should be sustained. The right to
     life, the obligation to sustain life,
     and passive euthanasia are discussed.

918 "Human life should be saved no matter how
     useless it becomes says French biologist
     Jean Rostand in his book, Humanly Possible,"
     THE NATIONAL OBSERVER. 4/7-13, 1973.

919 "Ite ad Joseph," COMMONWEAL. 49:363-364,
     January 21, 1949.
     An article on the 379 clergymen who
     sponsored a euthanasia bill in the New
     York legislature. The author is in dis-
     agreement with the clergymen.

920 "Killing of patients," BRITISH MEDICAL
     JOURNAL. 2:4-5, April 5, 1969.
     Voluntary euthanasia is termed the
     killing of patients instead of "the good
     death" according to those persons in
     opposition to the Euthanasia Bill.

921 "Letters," by N. Galloway. FORUM. 94:
     323-324, December, 1935.
     A letter written by a sufferer of an
     incurable disease in response to C. P.
     Gilman's article, "Right to die," FORUM.
     94:297-300. Galloway is basically in
     opposition to Gilman's views.

922 "Licensed to kill?" by Wallsend. CATHOLIC
     NURSE. 32:6-8, 1971.
     Any legislation which would enact
     voluntary euthanasia upon the elderly
     or infirmed is considered by this author

to be highly dangerous in the hands of a society which can manipulate legally within its legal statutes. The author also believes that under a euthanasia law, patients would feel obligated to die because they have become "a burden" to their families. In these cases, voluntary euthanasia becomes nothing more then licensed murder, and all efforts to legalize voluntary euthanasia should be spurned.

923 "Life is sacred," by J. J. Walsh. FORUM. 94:333-334, December, 1935.
Makes a distinction between the incurably ill, who is suffering, and the incurably neurotic, who wants a sympathetic ear. Asserts that the suffering individual wishes to grasp every second of life he or she has.

924 "Mercy killing," by J. B. Sheerin. CATHOLIC WORLD. 170:324-325, February, 1950.
The Catholic Church stands resolutely against any consideration of a patient as a mere social unit. Inherent dangers exist in considering a patient only in terms of his value to society and of the possibility of rehabilitation. Sheerin draws upon the World War II war crimes and other cases, such as that of Dr. Hermann Sander as a means of disclosing the inherent dangers that are present when mercy killings are allowed.

925 "Mongoloids and morality," AMERICA. 95: 608, September 29, 1956.
An argument to have the existence of mongoloids removed as a crutch for euthanasia is presented. An assertion is made that a cure for mongolism is just around the corner.

926 "Paul P. Krikorian, M. D., explains why
      why he prolongs life: because it is
      precious, every minute of it," THE
      NATIONAL OBSERVER. 4/1-12, 1972.

927 "Playing God," AMERICA. 107:1118,
      November 24, 1962.
         A critical analysis of the acquittal
      of the family at Liege, Belgium ... a
      distinction between abortion and eutha-
      nasia is mentioned.

928 "Politics of death," Russell Kirk.
      NATIONAL REVIEW. 23:315, March 23, 1971.
         Russell Kirk predicts that legalized
      euthanasia will enact an era of eminent
      doom for society. "If a social order
      fails to defend those who cannot defend
      themselves, then that order is impotent,
      or heartless, or both." p. 315

929 "Right and wrong of mercy killing; symposium-
      it's wrong to take human life ever,"
      LITERATY DIGEST. 124(23), October 23,
      1937.
         In this series of eight articles, it
      is asserted that man may use killing
      as an antedote. Suggests that the dying
      person is under emotional stress and his
      judgment is clouded. Claims that any-
      one assisting in mercy killing commits
      murder.

930 "The right to die," by M. R. Beard.
      FORUM. 94:323, December, 1935.
         Opposes C. P. Gilman's article, "Right
      to die," (FORUM. 94:297-300) which suggests
      that individuals have the right to take
      their own lives if they so choose.

931 "Right to die," by G. A. Lavy. LANCET.
      2:1363, December 26, 1970.
         Human life is sacred, and it is not
      for man to decide when it should close -

perhaps best states the position of this
very brief letter by G. A. Lavy.

932 "Right to die," by E. P. Scarlett.
GROUP PRACTICE. 18:65-67, July, 1969.
Studies the contemporary mood, criticism
of medical practices and several of the
euthanasia controversies. Emphasis is
placed on the "fundamental principles
of medicine."

933 "The right to die," by Zona Gale. FORUM.
95:110-112, April, 1936.
Argues against euthanasia and suicide.
Asserts that euthanasia is the "twin
brother" of suicide.

934 "Sacredness of life," by W. M. Abbott.
AMERICA. 108:326, March 9, 1963.
In a fifteen page pamphlet, Cardinal
Suenas devotes the bulk of his message
to confronting active euthanasia activists.
He contends that one dare not be a judge
on whom should live or die because each
life is sacred in that all are a part
of the Mystical Body of Christ.

935 "The sanctity of life," AMERICA. 101:
667, September 5, 1959.
Mr. Beavan's pragmatic reasoning is
questioned in this editorial written
after Mr. Beavan wrote an article which
appeared in the TIMES MAGAZINE on Sunday,
August 9, that describes his cool and
rational proposals for legalized euthanasia.

936 "Shall we legalize homicide?" OUTLOOK.
82:252-253, February 3, 1906.
In 1906, a bill was brought before the
Ohio Legislature recommending the legalization of euthanasia. Moral and ethical
arguments are raised against the widespread acceptance of euthanasia.

937 "Should we kill when we cannot cure?"
LITERARY DIGEST. 47:627, October 11,
1913.
The author of this article equates
euthanasia with murder and believes that
physicians have no right to take another's
life. Under no circumstances should the
murder-euthanasia of humans be considered,
emphasizes the author.

938 "Some non-religious views against proposed
mercy killing legislation," by Yale
Komisar. MINNESOTA LAW REVIEW. 42:
969-1042, May, 1958.
Raises objections to the legalization
of voluntary euthanasia. For related
information see also: Williams.
MINNESOTA LAW REVIEW. November, 1958.

939 "Vexing problems in forensic medicine,"
by I. Phillips Frohman. NEW YORK
UNIVERSITY LAW REVIEW. 31:1215-1222,
1956.
Objects to the American Euthanasia
Bill and questions the true mercy of
euthanasia acts.

940 "Why I oppose mercy killings," by B. F.
Miller. WOMAN'S HOME COMPANION. 77:
38-39, June, 1950.
Considers mercy killing a backward-
looking operation which leads medical
science down blind alleys. The arguments supporting euthanasia to relieve
suffering are thwarted by examples of
medical mis-diagnosis, and advances
in modern research.

941 "Why I oppose mercy killings by B. F.
Miller - discussion," WOMAN'S HOME
COMPANION. 77:14, August, 1950.
Six letters are presented expressing
varied views concerning Miller's
opposition to euthanasia.

NEWSPAPER ARTICLES

942 "Cardinal Cooke restates his opposition
to euthanasia at service honoring three
hundred couples from New York City,
Metropolitan area who will celebrate their
50th Wedding Anniversaries in 1974,"
NEW YORK TIMES. 31:7, January 14, 1974.

943 "Doctor wants mercy killings ruled illegal,"
THE GREENVILLE NEWS. 291:5, October 18,
1974.
   While in some cases mercy killings may
be morally acceptable, Dr. Robert M.
Vestch said that he believes such killings
should be outlawed.

944 "Letter scares O. R. Russell. February 14
article on right of patient with terminal
illness to chose death; contends euthanasia law of anykind is inviting disaster,"
NEW YORK TIMES. 36:4, March 10, 1972.

945 "Norfolk, Mass. Prison colony wins debate
on issue against Williams College,"
NEW YORK TIMES. 17:8, October 9, 1951.

946 "Opposed by NYS Hi-Y Club," NEW YORK TIMES.
26:1, December 11, 1939.

947 "Reply to anonymous doctor's letter opposes
mercy killing," NEW YORK TIMES. 26:6,
March 1, 1950

948 "World Medical Association condemns practice
under any circumstances," NEW YORK TIMES.
22:4, October 18, 1950.

949   "Biologist reflects on old age and death,"
      by F. B. Sumner. SCIENTIFIC MONTHLY.
      61:143-149, August, 1945.
      "One of the most pathetic and curious
    facts of human existence is the tenacity
    with which most persons cling to life,
    however tragic ... and however pain-
    ful in the last stages. The patient ...
    fights ... for life." p. 147

950   "Corrective surgery in elderly patients;
      a dilemma," by D. C. McGoon. MINNESOTA
      MEDICINE. 52:1633, October, 1969.
    The advances in medical science
    prevent the issue of euthanasia from
    being further deferred. A majority of
    physicians presently practice modified
    forms of euthanasia by withholding
    treatment from the most pitiful of the
    aged or infirm.

951   "Death is man's friend, not foe," MED-
      ICAL WORLD NEWS. 9:62, passim, September
      20, 1968.
    Advancing life-expectancies may prove
    to be man's foe and not his friend.
    The author presents two basic ideas -
    the first idea is that our present
    practice of applying to the old all life-
    saving drugs and techniques does the old
    themselves an ultimate disservice. The
    second is that this misuse of medical
    skill is aggravating the population
    imbalance.

952   "Dying with dignity," by C. W. Letourneau.
      HOSPITAL MANAGEMENT. 109:27, passim,
      June, 1970.
    Is the prolongation of life after
    eighty good or bad for society? Dr.
    Letourneau debates this issue and also
    gives the pros and cons of voluntary
    euthanasia for the aged or those suffer-
    ing from an irremediable condition.

953 "Elderly at the end of life," by W. F.
   Anderson. NURSING TIMES. 69:193-194,
   February 8, 1973.
      Introduces the concept of "medicated
   manslaughter"; and aspects of an elderly
   patient's life as death approaches is
   discussed. Anderson asserts that one
   may seek a merciful release during
   periods of excrutiating pain, even when
   an illness is not terminal.

954 "Ethical questions in geriatric care.
   Rights and obligations of elderly patients.
   Part 2," by J. Agate. NURSING MIRROR
   AND MIDWIVES JOURNAL. 133:42-43, November 12, 1971.
      Discusses the right of sick, elderly
   patients and the obligations of those who
   attend the elderly. Geriatric care and
   management is largely a question of
   individual circumstance and the maintenance of a quality of life after
   successful treatment.

955 "Euthanasia," by J. Scoffern. BELGRAVIA.
   7:221-224, (1868-1869).
      Describes euthanasia as death without
   disease, free from pain and reveals
   modes of longevity and describes his
   idea of the good life.

   ALSO IN: CANADIAN MONTHLY AND NATIONAL
   REVIEW. 2:461-464, 1872.

956 "Euthanasia at eighty? proposal by British
   Health Officer," NEWSWEEK. 73:77,
   May 12, 1969.

957 "Euthanasia from Scoffern's Stray Leaves of
   Science and Folk-Lore," CANADIAN MONTHLY
   AND NATIONAL REVIEW. 2:461-466, 1872.
      Describes euthanasia as death with-
   out disease and also describes modes of

longevity. Points out specific instances
of longevity and describes the good life.

ALSO IN: BELGRAVIA. 7:221-228, 1868-
1869.

958 "Euthanasia pill to allow elderly death
with dignity," AMERICAN DRUGGIST. 166:
8, July 25, 1972.

959 "Geriatric hazards," by W. Schwartz and A.
T. Papas. JOURNAL OF THE AMERICAN
GERIATRIC SOCIETY. 15:936-940, October,
1967.

960 "Give me one more pill, resident asks, and
the right to die at my discretion,"
by E. M. Garman. MODERN NUSRING HOME.
31:46-47, September, 1973.

961 "Illinois association of Homes for the
Aging speaker·warns administrators to
brace for more liability regarding
life maintenance," MODERN NURSING
HOME. 28:42, May, 1972.
   The Illinois Association is concerned
with the legal reprocussions the administration of a nursing home face in dealing
with the life-death decisions of his
charges.

962 "Many individuals can recover from old
age - interview," by J. Brantner.
GERIATRICS. 24:48, passim, May, 1969.
   An interview with Dr. Brantner provides
the reader with the personal viewpoints
of this clinical pathologist. Dr.
Brantner has conducted extensive research
on death and aging, and some of his
comments are very elucidating on this
controversial subject.

963 "Old lady slept," NEWSWEEK. 53:44, May 18, 1959.
 An 80-year-old woman, dying with cancer, slept, with the aid of her physician, until she died. NEWSWEEK reporters discuss the resultant controversy and public reaction.

964 "Old people's adjustment to life and their struggle against death," by E. Qvarnstrom. NORDISK MEDICIN. 11:2591-2595, September 13, 1941.

965 "Older persons look at death," by H. Feifel. GERIATRICS. 11:127-130, March 1956.
 The purpose of this study is to present some data regarding the conscious attitudes of persons 65 years of age and older regarding death. The subjects consist of 40 white males living at a Veteran's Administration Domicilary. Results are given on a percentage basis.

966 "Problem of physician responsibility: negative attitudes toward care of the aged," by C. H. Kramer and G. F. Johnston. PROFESSIONAL NURSING HOME. 7:54, passim, August, 1965.

967 "Problems created by medical progress: what do you do for the aged - and when do you stop doing?" MEDICAL WORLD NEWS. 13:42-55, April 7, 1972.
 Medical science has been able to increase life expectancies of women by 16 years and men by 13 years. Duke University conducted a study of aging; some of its findings are reported. Medical advances and education in the area of skilled care for the elderly are needed, and one hopes foresight will be shown in this area in the future.

968 "Terminal illness in the aged," by Exton-
Smith. THE LANCET. August 3, 1961.
States that in a study of 220 patients
dying in London geriatric hospital,
eleven continually expressed a wish to
die.

969 "Views of the aged on the timing of death,"
by C. E. Preston and R. H. Williams.
GERONTOLOGIST. 11:300-304, Winter,
1971. (Pt. 1)
Veterans and nursing home subjects
were interviewed concerning their
preferences for negative and positive
euthanasia. Half rejected withholding
of life-sustaining or life-shortening
prodecures; and one quarter rejected
life-shortening but favored omission of
life-sustaining measures; while one-third
favored death through either omission
or commission. The subjects attitudes
are correlated with their quality of
currently maintained existence.

970 "Who should live?" by G. W. Paulson.
GERIATRICS. 28:132-136, March, 1973.
"When the physician holds a patient's
life in the balance are heroic efforts
always justified? This article reviews
selected ethical problems in medical
gerontology, and two representative
cases emphasize problems related to
support of life for the aged." p. 132.
On the last page of the article, six
partial solutions to some of the ethical
dilemmas are proposed.

SEE ALSO:
TERMINAL PATIENT CARE

971   "Aided suicide among eskimos," TIME.
      54:40, September 19, 1949.
      Aided suicide has long been the
custom among eskimos. The case involving the mercy killing - aided
suicide - of a tuberculin woman of 45
is reported. The subesquent murder
trial of the woman's son who aided her
in her death and the subsequent verdict
of that trial are also reported.

972   "Another modest proposal," by Ferdinand
      Mount. NATIONAL REVIEW. 20:233, 257.
      March 12, 1968.
      A modest proposal is presented - a
termination of existence bill. Under the
provisions of this bill, an individual
over the age of 21 could request that
his life be ended efficiently, painlessly,
and without charge. A detailed analysis
of this legislative program is reported.

973   "Antidysthanasia contracts: a proposal
      for legalizing death with dignity,"
      PACIFIC LAW JOURNAL. 5:738-763, July,
      1974.

974   "Application of the Presidents and Directors
      of Georgetown College (1964) 331F. 2d.
      1000 (D. C. Cir). Cert. denied. 377US.
      978.

975   "Bill in the New York Legislature,"
      COMMONWEAL. 29:422-423, February 10,
      1939.

976   "Bill to kill: poem," by R. K. Munkithick.
      HARPER'S WEEKLY. 50:709, May 19, 1906.
      A poem concerning a proposed eutha-
nasia bill. The poem ends, "Tis very rough/
And quite enough/ To kill the bill to kill."

977 "British humanists seek mercy killing,"
    THE CATHOLIC BANNER. 6(41):8, Novem-
    ber 21, 1974.
       Analyzes what seems to be a first
    move in the long-expected drive by
    British humanists to legalize eutha-
    nasia on the eve of Parliament's
    opening.

978 "Case for voluntary euthanasia," by M.
    M. Moore. UMKC LAW REVIEW. 42:327-
    340, Spring, 1974.

979 "A cause of action for 'wrong life',"
    MINNESOTA LAW REVIEW. 55:58, 1970.

980 "Changing concepts of death - editorial,"
    HAWAII MEDICAL JOURNAL. 30:278, July-
    August, 1971
       Voices support for the legal pro-
    tection of the physician, who wishes
    to respect his patient's express desire
    not to have his life maintained when
    it has become hopelessly meaningless.

981 "Contemporary medical treatment: the
    State's interest re-evaluated,"
    MINNESOTA LAW REVIEW. 293 (1966).

982 "Controversial euthanasia bill introduced
    in Maryland," by R. W. Stratton.
    HOSPITAL PROGRESS. 55:21, April, 1974.
       Senator Julian L. Lapides introduced
    a bill in the Maryland General Assembly
    which would give legal force to an
    individual's request that no heroic
    measures be used to prolong his life.
    The bill is opposed by Lawrence Cardinal
    Shehan on the grounds that it does not
    provide for a dignified death for those
    who have not signed the document.

983 "Court required extraordinary means to
prolong life: Miami, Florida,"
HOSPITAL PROGRESS. 52:19, August,
1971.
A Dade County circuit court rules that
a physician must use every effort possible
to sustain life in a terminally ill
patient.

984 "Criminal law - euthanasia - defendant
allowed to withdraw guilty plea of
manslaughter to accommodate finding of
not guilty on arraignment," NOTRE
DAME LAW. 34:460, passim, May, 1959.
Reports findings in the case of People
vs Werner. Criminal #58-3636, Cook
County Court, Illinois, December 30, 1958.

985 "Criminal omissions," by Kirchheimer. HAR-
VARD LAW REVIEW. 55:615, 625-628, 1942.
Discusses the traditional relationship
between the physician and the patient.
Claims there exists a legal duty to act
upon the part of the physician, and any
failure to act may be looked upon as
a criminal omission.

986 "Criminal omissions," by Russell. YALE LAW
JOURNAL. 67:590, 599-600, 1958.
Describes how commission of criminal
homicide by omission of treatment is
treated.

987 "Dawson of Penn, Lord. HOUSE OF LORDS PAR-
LIAMENTARY DEBATES--EUTHANASIA BILL.
vol. 103, p. 480. London:HMSO, 1936.

988 "Death, legal and illegal; excerpts from
'Death by choice'," by D. C. Maguire.
ATLANTIC MONTHLY. 233:72-74+, February,
1974.

989 "Death of a son," by P. D. Sholin. READER'S
DIGEST. 94:141-144, January, 1969.

"There is no need to prolong life
beyond the point where the patient can
respond to his environment." (p. 141)
A minister-father discusses his severely
brain-damaged infant son and the
decision not to prolong a hopeless life.
Some suggestions of legislation are also
analyzed.

990 "Death with dignity," by W. W. Sackett, Jr.,
SOUTHERN MEDICAL JOURNAL. 64:330-332,
March, 1971.
A paper read before a meeting of the
Southern Medical Association, 1969,
in which Sackett proposes to physicians
that they permit the hopelessly ill
patient to die with dignity and not
prolong his life when it has reached a
meaningless state. He additionally
mentions Florida Legislation.

991 "Death with dignity: a legislative
necessity," by W. W. Sackett. JOURNAL
OF THE FLORIDA MEDICAL ASSOCIATION.
61:366-367, May, 1974.
Points out the reasons which make
euthanasia legislation's enactment seem
of paramount importance.

992 "Death with dignity legislation: it really
isn't necessary," by F. J. Evans.
JOURNAL OF THE FLORIDA MEDICAL ASSOCIATION.
61:363-365, May, 1974.
Argues that the Florida euthanasia
legislative bill would be ineffective.
The ultimate decision would not be made
by legislative action, for professional
judgment cannot be legislated. The
vague and confusing bill enhances the
possibility of malpractice suits, Evans
asserts.

993 "Death with dignity: the debate goes on,"
SCIENCE NEWS. 102:118, August 19, 1972.

Walter Sackett introduced a bill into the Florida Legislature concerning death with dignity. The living will document's terms of consent are disclosed.

994 "Definition of irreversible coma as a criterion for death," JOURNAL OF THE AMERICAN MEDICAL ASSOCIATION. 205: 337-340, August 5, 1968.

This report of the Ad Hoc Committee of the Harvard Medical School examines the definition of brain death. Discussions of unreceptivity and unresponsivity; no movement or breathing; no reflexes; flat electroencephalogram are used as a means of concluding that death as an event has taken place. A section of this article is devoted to legal commentary. In this section, the case of Thomas vs Anderson and Smith vs Smith are examined. Additionally a commentary on Pope Puis XII's The Prolongation of Life is included.

995 "Dilemma in dying," TIME. 98:44, July 19, 1971.

Carmen Martinez pleaded for a peaceful death. Dr. Lopez was in a dilemma about withholding life-sustaining treatment, which only prolonged the agony of her dying. Judge David Potter ruled that Mrs. Martinez could not be forced to accept treatment that was painful, and the transfusions were stopped.

996 "Do patients ever have rights in the timing of their own death? When is it time to die" Prolegomenon to voluntary euthanasia? Dying person - his plight, his right," by M. T. Sullivan, et al. NEW ENGLAND LAW REVIEW. 8:181, passim, Spring, 1973.

997 "The dying and their treatment in Jewish law," by I. Jakobovits. HEBREW MEDICAL JOURNAL. 2:242-251, 1961. Also in: 2:104-114, 1961. (Hebrew)

998 "Dying patient: a qualified right to refuse medical treatment," by D. J. Davis. JOURNAL OF FAMILY LAW. 7: 644, 658, Winter, 1968.
Discusses the idea of having compelled medical treatment against the expressed wishes of the patient.

999 "The dying patient, the doctor and the law," by J. Russell Elkenton. VILLA-NOVA LAW REVIEW. 13(4):740-743, Summer, 1968.
States that in allowing the patient to die, the physician should assume no responsibility. Extenuating circum-stances such as age and range of human activity are emphasized when faced with a euthanasia situation.

1000 "Euthanasia," ECLECTIC MAGAZINE. 138: 683-685, 1901-1902.
Suggests that a certain amount of distrust will develop among the public for physicians should the doctors openly vie for euthanasia. States that patients will ultimately seek physicians who respect human life. Included also are references to pro-posed euthanasia legislation.
Also in: SPECTATOR. 88:134-35, January 25, 1902.

1001 "Euthanasia," NURSING MIRROR AND MIDWIVES JOURNAL. 128:14, April 4, 1969.
A parliamentary correspondent reports on the opinions of some of its Lords and Ladies concerning the Voluntary Euthanasia Bill which was rejected by the House of Lords.

1002 "Euthanasia," SPECTATOR. 88:134-135,
January 25, 1902.
Suggests that a certain amount of
distrust for physicians will develop
among the public should doctors openly
vie for euthanasia. States that
patients will seek physicians who respect
life. Also, presents information concerning contemporary euthanasia legislation.

Also in: ECLECTIC MAGAZINE. 138:683-685,
1901-1902.

1003 "Euthanasia," by A. L. Banks. BULLETIN
OF THE NEW YORK ACADEMY OF MEDICINE.
26(5):297-305, May, 1950.
In the latter half of the 19th Century,
articles on euthanasia were appearing
in such journals as FORTNIGHTLY REVIEW
(1873) and SPECTATOR (1873) asserting
that the subject must be reviewed
for reform "at a latter date". As
early as 1936, efforts were undertaken
to legalize euthanasia. From the legal
standpoint, euthanasia is murder. Med-
ically, physicians in the House of Lords
are against the practice. These legislators assert that what is incurable
today, may be curable tomorrow. The
dying patient's primary concern is not
demanding euthanasia; but rather, he
is chiefly concerned with the relief of
pain, good nursing, and friendly care.

1004 "Euthanasia," by Brock. PROCEEDINGS
OF THE ROYAL SOCIETY OF MEDICINE.
63:659-663, July, 1970.
At the October 13, 1969 meeting,
the subject of euthanasia legislation
from 1936 to date was reviewed.
Presented were pro and con agruments,
justificating arguments and the desir-
ability of euthanasia legislation.

1005   "Euthanasia," by H. Roberts. NEW STATES-
       MAN AND NATION. 10:630-631, November
       2, 1935.
          Those forms of active euthanasia
       used to relieve the pain and suffering
       of the terminal cancer patient find
       support as well as a forewarning of
       possible legal implications.

1006   "Euthanasia," by Glanville L. Williams.
       MEDICO-LEGAL JOURNAL. 41:14-34, 1973.
          Williams, a long-time supporter of
       the euthanasia movement has "long
       ceased to believe that ... a rational
       argument can convince those who approach
       (euthanasia) with a firm rejection."
       He has found most arguments against it
       too superficial to mention but does
       state that the doctor's fear "is that
       any legislation would be hedged about
       by unacceptable conditions." However,
       Williams points out that the legalization
       of euthanasia might make some individuals
       aware that they have some self-determin-
       ing rights. The concept of omissions
       is discussed in the light of malformed
       children. Medical treatment and the
       consent of the patient; the dangers of
       honesty; the right to commit suicide;
       and when there is a right to prevent
       an act of suicide are also topics in-
       cluded in Williams' discussion. The
       rationale for assisting a suicide and
       the legal status of such acts are
       analyzed as well as the reasons in-
       volved in failing to prevent a suicide
       examined.

1007   "Euthanasia - a question of right versus
       justice," by S. Rusoen. NORDISK
       MEDICIN (Stockholm) 89:131-132, May,
       1974. (Norwegian)

THE LAW AND EUTHANASIA

1008   "Euthanasia: a study in comparative
         criminal law,"   by H. Silving.
         UNIVERSITY OF PENNSYLVANIA LAW REVIEW.
         103:350-389, December, 1954.
           A comparative study of suicide as
         well as a direct mercy killing study
         as each relate to the criminal law
         is reviewed.

1009   "Euthanasia and biathanasia: on dying
         and killing,"   by D. W. Louisell.
         CATHOLIC UNIVERSITY LAW REVIEW.   22:
         723-745, Summer, 1973.

1010   "Euthanasia and murder,"   by C. K. Chester-
         ton.   AMERICAN LAW REVIEW.   8:486,490,
         1937.
           Chesterton recognizes some potential
         problems with the legalization of
         voluntary euthanasia.   Careful watch
         must be kept on the legal machinery,
         he suggests.

1011   "Euthanasia and related problems in
         Swedish law,"   by Hans Thornstedt.
         ZEITSCHRIFT FUER RECHTSMEDIZIN (West
         Germany).   70(1):32-35, 1972.
           In Sweden, active euthanasia is illegal
         and considered as murder.   In certain
         cases, however, a lenient punishment
         or no punishment is given   the defendant.
         Acceleration   of death by pain-killing
         methods in hopeless cases is legal.
         Such treatment is considered to be
         passive euthanasia.

1012   "Euthanasia and the care of the dying,"
         by S. Bok.   BIOSCIENCE.   23:461-466,
         August, 1973.
           S. Bok begins by defining euthanasia
         from various sources; these definitions
         reflect many differences which
         prevail when such a definition is
         attempted.   Legal proposals (with cases

cited), and analysis of the growing concern over dying, dilemmas of the physician including treatment and/or lack of treatment; and patient care are examined. Also, a reflection on social norms is presented.

1013 "Euthanasia and the law," NEWSWEEK. 83:45, January 29, 1974.

1014 "Euthanasia and the right to die - moral, ethical and legal perspectives," by B. Vodiga. CHI-KENT LAW REVIEW. 51:1-40, Summer, 1974.

1015 "Euthanasia: criminal, tort, constitutional and legislative considerations," NOTRE DAME LAW. 48:1202-1260, June, 1973.

1016 "Euthanasia in Hadamar Sanatorium and international law," by M. K. Dessler. JOURNAL OF CRIMINAL LAW. 43:735-755, March-April, 1953.

1017 "Euthanasia - legal aspects," by V. C. Allred. LINACRE QUARTERLY. 14(2): 1-15, April, 1947.
A treatise on the legal aspects of euthanasia is presented. Cases involving mercy killings, suicide pacts, abortion, and duelling are discussed, and the legal guild involved in each case is explained. Legal definitions and statutes are quoted. Also, a short discussion of natural law and divine law is included.

1018 "Euthanasia (legislation)," LAW TIMES. 182:412-413, November 28, 1936.

1019 "Euthanasia: no present future," MEDICAL WORLD NEWS. 14:5-6, March 23, 1973.
Recently in the state of Oregon, a positive euthanasia bill was introduced

into the state's legislature. The
public reaction was against the adoption
of this bill. Here is an explanation
of opposing views and a "gestimation"
as to where euthanasia legislation
is headed.

1020   "Euthanasia: none dare call it murder,"
        by Joseph Sanders. JOURNAL OF CRIMINAL
        LAW, CRIMINOLOGY AND POLICE SCIENCE.
        60(3):351-359, September, 1960.
          The case of a college student who
        euthanized his mother who was suffering
        from leukemia is used to launch a
        discussion of the legalization of eutha-
        nasia. Suggestions are offered on
        those patients for whom euthanasia should
        be provided. There exists strong
        opposition to the legalization of volun-
        tary euthanasia from religious leaders
        and others. And Sanders points out
        that support for a change in euthanasia
        legislation lacks sufficient organi-
        zation.

1021   "Euthanasia: the individual's right to
        freedom of choice," SUFFOLK UNIVERSITY
        LAW REVIEW. 5:190, Fall, 1970.

1022   "Folk rationalizations in the unwritten
        law," by R. B. Vance and W. Wynne, Jr.
        AMERICAN JOURNAL OF SOCIOLOGY. 39:
        483-492, January, 1934.

1023   "Higher charity: proposed legalization of
        voluntary euthanasia," SURVEY. 68:
        322-323, July 15, 1932.
          For a voluntary euthanasia plan to
        be successful, rules and guidelines
        must be established. For a euthanasia
        act to become effective, these guide-
        lines must be followed. An analysis of
        these guidelines is presented.

1024 "Human drama in death and taxes," by J.
      Fisher. TRUSTS AND ESTATES.
      112:428, June, 1973.

1025 "Illinois Association of Homes for the
      Aging speaker warns administration
      to brace for more liability regarding
      life maintenance," MODERN NURSING
      HOME. 28:42, May, 1972.
        The Illinois Association is concerned
      with the legal reprocussions the
      administrator of a nursing home faces
      in dealing with life-death decisions
      of his charges.

1026 "Indictment for euthanasia dismissed,"
      LAKARTIDNINGEN. 62:500-504, February
      17, 1965. (Swedish)

1027 "Informed consent and the dying patient,"
      YALE LAW REVIEW. 83:1632-1634, July,
      1974.

1028 "Is there a right to die? - a study of the
      law on euthanasia," by E. J. Gurney.
      CUMBER-SAM LAW REVIEW. 2:235, Summer,
      1972.

1029 "Is this legislation really necessary?"
      by Franklin J. Evans. JOURNAL OF THE
      FLORIDA MEDICAL ASSOCIATION. 59:51-
      53, March, 1972.
        Strongly opposes death with dignity
      legislation, not through the conceptual
      idea but on the grounds that such
      legislation is useless.

1030 "Ite ad Joseph," COMMONWEAL. 49:363-364,
      January 21, 1949.
        An attack on the 379 clergymen who
      sponsored a euthanasia bill in the New
      York Legislature. The author is in dis-
      agreement with the clergymen.

1031   "It's illegal to die," SCIENCE DIGEST.
       74:52, December, 1973.

1032   "Jewish attitudes toward euthanasia," by
       F. Rosner. NEW YORK STATE JOURNAL
       OF MEDICINE. 67:2499-2506, September
       15, 1967.
          After a discussion of terminology
       and various definitions, a brief intro-
       duction to euthanasia societies and some
       reasons for such societies' existence,
       the author launches into a discussion
       of the legal attitudes toward eutha-
       nasia. In addition to defining and
       explaining the Jewish attitudes toward
       euthanasia, the pros and cons and
       protestant and catholic attitudes are
       examined. Excellent bibliography at
       end of article.

1033   "John F. Kennedy Memorial Hospital
       v. Heston (1970) 58N. J. 576, 279,
       Atl. 2d. 670."

1034   "Legal aspects of euthanasia," ALBANY
       LAW REVIEW. 36:674, 1972.

1035   "Legal aspects of euthanasia, " by J.
       Ekelmans. NEDERLANDS TIJDSCHRIFT
       VOOR GENEESKUNDE. (Amsterdam) 116:
       1096-1102, June 24, 1972. (Dutch)

1036   "Legal aspects of euthanasia - the
       criminal law 70202 and euthanasia,"
       by M. Suzuki. COMPREHENSIVE NURSING
       QUARTERLY. 4:99-111, Summer, 1969.
       (Japanese)
          M. Suzuki discusses euthanasia as it
       directly relates to criminal law 70202.
       Included are the legal implications
       of the practice of euthanasia.

THE LAW AND EUTHANASIA

1037 "The legal aspects of medical euthanasia,"
      by D. W. Meyers. BIOSCIENCE. 23:
      467-470, August, 1973.
      After an analysis of the implications
      of the term, euthanasia, the affirmative
      act of causing death is examined in
      detail. Other aspects of euthanasia,
      such as withholding treatment or terminat-
      ing ordinary medical treatment and
      extraordinary means are discussed.

1038 "Legal aspects of the decision not to
      prolong life," by G. P. Fletcher.
      JOURNAL OF THE AMERICAN MEDICAL
      ASSOCIATION. 203:65-68, January 1,
      1968.
      Describes the legal consequences
      of life-prolongation. Acts and omissions
      are discussed with reference made to
      the Sander case (the injection of 40 cc
      of air into the veins of a terminally
      ill cancer patient by her physician).
      Additionally, makes distinctions between
      the law in theory and law in action.

1039 "Legal aspects of the decision not to use
      extreme measures to prolong life,"
      by H. Creighton. SUPERVISOR NURSE. 3:
      50, passim, July, 1972.
      Helen Creighton's work cites state-
      ments by numerous authorities concerning
      various aspects of euthanasia and the
      various types of death. In her con-
      cluding statements, she proposes that
      it should be the physician's duty to
      evaluate forseeable candidates for
      cardiac resuscitation and supply specific
      written orders as to what means should
      be employed in case of heart stoppage.
      If medical orders are not available,
      she believes that the medical personnel
      should be guided by the ethics set
      forth in this discussion.

168

1040   "Legal aspects relating to euthanasia,"
       by C. E. Orth, Jr. MARYLAND STATE
       MEDICAL JOURNAL. 2(3):120-128, March,
       1953.
          Presents an indepth analysis of the
       problem of euthanasia. Legal definitions
       of such terms as murder and malice
       are developed. The 1939 Euthanasia
       Society of America Bill and various
       other euthanasia legislations are dis-
       cussed. Orth assumes the format of a
       script centered around two central
       characters - Mr. Layman and Mr. Lawyer.
       From these two characters are pivoted
       lay and legal viewpoints of the eutha-
       nasia controversy.

1041   "Legal questions pertaining to euthanasia,"
       by J. F. Rang. TIJDSCHRIFT VOOR
       ZIEKENVERPLEGING. 25:300-304, March 28,
       1972. (Dutch)

1042   "Legal right of the patient to a death
       worthy of a human being," by W.
       Uhlenbruck. THERAPIE DER GEGEN-
       WART. (Berlin) 113:127-129, passim,
       January, 1974. (German)

1043   "Legalization of voluntary euthanasia,"
       by R. Harding. NINETEENTH CENTURY AND
       AFTER. 124:238-248, August, 1938.

1044   "Legalize euthanasia," by Wolbarst THE
       FORUM. 94:330-332, 1935.

1045   "Licensed to kill?" by Wallsend. CATHOLIC
       NURSE. 32:6-8, 1971.
          Any legislation which would enact
       voluntary euthanasia upon the elderly
       or infirmed is considered by this
       author to be highly dangerous in the
       hands of a society which can manipulate
       legally within legal statutes. The

author also believes that under a
euthanasia law, patients would feel
obligated to die because they have
become a "burden" to their families.
In these cases, voluntary euthanasia
becomes nothing more than licensed
murder, and all efforts to legalize
voluntary euthanasia should be spurned.

1046 "Liege trial and the problem of voluntary
euthanasia," by L. Colbrook. LANCET.
2:1225-1226, December 8, 1962. Also
editorial: p. 1205.
"The Euthanasia Society believes that
the time has come for a serious reappraisal of the advantages and difficulties
and possible dangers that might result
from the legalization of voluntary
euthanasia. In a recent publication,
A Plan for Voluntary Euthanasia, the
Society put forward proposals that it
commends to both laymen and medical
staff." (p. 1225).

1047 "Life and death of the law," by D. J.
Keefe. HOSPITAL PROGRESS. 53:64-74,
March, 1972.
Father Keefe, a lawyer and priest,
presents both theological and legislative arguments surrounding life, death,
and the law. Treats legal rationality
and freedom; the Judeo-Christian
tension between rationality and freedom;
law in service of myth; the failure of
the utopian rationalization of man;
the mutability of myth; the liturgy of
civil religion; a problem for theo-
logians (civil and otherwise); facing
the people; law - fallen and unfallen;
messianism - the alternative to historical determinism; Sacramental law as
Christian witness; freedom of worship
and loyalty and explores pacifism.

1048 "Lords reject voluntary euthanasia,"
     NURSING TIMES. 65:446, April 3, 1969.
       The Voluntary Euthanasia Bill, 1969,
     was rejected by 61 votes to 40 votes
     by the House of Lords on March 25,
     1969. Many Lords and Ladies comment
     on the bill.

1049 "Make it legal," TIME. 48:70, November 18,
     1946.
       Dr. Robert Latou Dickinson made an
     attempt to have euthanasia legalized.
     The result, reported here, was a
     furious public reaction.

1050 "Martin v Commonwealth (1946) Va. 1009,
     1018, 1019, 37 SE 2d43,47."
       From article footnote: "The consent
     of a victim does not change the character-
     ization of the homicide from murder to
     any lesser crime."

1051 "Mechanism of certain forms of death in
     medicolegal practice," by E. Gardner.
     MEDICO-LEGAL AND CRIMINOLOGICAL
     REVIEW. 10:120-133, July, 1942.

1052 "Medicine and euthanasia," by L. Portes.
     BULLETIN DEL' ORDRE DES MEDECINS.
     85-100, March, 1951.
       Portes begins with a historical
     analysis of euthanasia. After which,
     laws and legislation in many of the
     states of the United States beginning
     with the first legal text concerning
     euthanasia on a proposition by Ann
     Hall to the Ohio Legislature are examined.
     Cases are mentioned. Questions are
     raised concerning the care of the dying
     and the idea of euthanasia by consent.
     Suggests that the subject of euthanasia
     is a very difficult one to resolve.

1053 "Mercy killing advocates of America and
Brittain form organization," NEWS-
WEEK. 11:26, January 31, 1938.
Seeing a loved one die a lingering
death with a painful illness is
alarming. Suggests in such instances
that euthanasia may appear a reasonable alternative. Cases are cited as
well as legislation briefly discussed.

1054 "Mercy killing legislation - a rejoinder to;
some non-religious views against proposed
mercy killing legislation," by Glanville L. Williams. MINNESOTA LAW REVIEW.
43:1-12, November, 1958.
Responds to the objections raised by
Yale Komisar to the legalization of
voluntary euthanasia. See Also:
Komisar. MINNESOTA LAW REVIEW, May,
1958.

1055 "Morals, medicine and the law - a symposium," NEW YORK UNIVERSITY LAW
REVIEW. 31:1157, passim, November,
1956.
The articles comprising this symposium are: "The issues - introduction,"
by T. A. Cowan; "An ethic of freedom:
a philosopher's view," by H. M. Kallen;
"Freedom and order before God - a
Catholic view," by J. D. Hassett; "Freedom and responsibility in medical and
sex ethics; a protestant view," by P.
Ramsey; and "Morality in medico-legal
problems: a Jewish view," by E.
Rachman. Also contained are special
articles: "Vexing problems in forensic
medicine: a physician's view," by J.
P. Frohman; "A special corner of civil
liberties: a legal view," by H. Kalven,
Jr.,; and "The place of law in medico-
moral problems: a legal view," by M.
Ploscowe.

1056 "Murder from the best of motives," LAW
QUARTERLY. 5:188, 1889.
A physician admits practicing euthanasia
on terminally ill patients during his
career in medical practice.

1057 "Murder or mercy?" TIME. 55:20-21, June
5, 1950.
Eugene Braunsdorff shot his retarded
daughter out of an act of mercy. The
court judged differently.

1058 "Non-finisher," ECONOMIST. 230:24,
March 29, 1969.
Asserts one major objection to Lord
Reglan's euthanasia bill - the Christian
ethic.

1059 "Obligation to live versus option to die,"
by S. M. Simons. SOUTHERN MEDICAL
JOURNAL. 65:731-757, June, 1972.
Simon discusses the legal aspects
of euthanasia and analyzes the ethics
of prolonging life in the case of a
terminal illness as well as the responsibility of the physician in such instances.

1060 "On the question of prolonging life,"
by N. Hershey. AMERICAN JOURNAL OF
NURSING. 71:521-522, March, 1971.
The role of the nurse in the care
of the terminally ill patient is a
delicately important one. The nurse
must abide by the attending physician's
orders, which, in some cases, may have
legal complications. When the nurse
feels that the physician's decision
is in error and fails bringing it to
the attention of someone in authority,
he or she may be subject to criminal
prosecution. With the creation of a
committee to aid in the decision process,
these problems diminish.

1061 "On tort liability for 'wrongful' life,"
      by G. Tedeschi.   ISR. LAW REVIEW.
      1:513, 1966.
        Discusses the idea that certain
      circumstances of existence are in
      and of themselves tort or injury to
      the person alive.

1062 "Oregon bishops score euthanasia bill,"
      HOSPITAL PROGRESS.   54:96c, March,
      1973.
        The bishops of Oregon denounce a legis-
      lative proposal that would legalize
      active euthanasia. The euthanasia pro-
      posal, Senate Bill 179, would allow
      persons suffering from an "incurable
      condition" to request administration
      of euthanasia.

1063 "Palm Springs General Hospital v Martinez.
      July, 1971. Circuit Court #71-12687,
      Miami."
        Case involves the daughter of a 72-
      year old patient being allowed to refuse
      surgery for her mother.

1064 "Power to kill; homicide as euthanasia,"
      by M. Evans. AMERICAN OPINION. 17:
      39-41, passim, January, 1974.
        Offers a reflection on the inconsis-
      tencies in the public's attitude toward
      abortion and euthanasia. Evans reviews
      the implications of governmental
      implementation of euthanasia and draws
      considerable argumental reference from
      the Commandment: Thou shall not kill."

1065 "The principle of euthanasia," by G. N.
      Anthony. PLAIN VIEW. 11:188-204,
      November, 1957.
        Favors establishing a legal right to
      practice euthanasia.

1066 "Prolonging life," by G. P. Fletcher.
      WASHINGTON LAW REVIEW. 42:999, June,
      1967.

1067 "Questions of life or death?" by N.
      Hershey. AMERICAN JOURNAL OF NURSING.
      68:1910-1912, September, 1968.
      "While it is not the nurse's decision
      when to use modern technology to pro-
      long life and when to omit or dis-
      continue it, she does have certain
      ethical and legal problems in regard
      to such decisions. Definitive legal
      guidelines that physicians and nurses
      can use if and when they come, will
      be based on standards devised by the
      medical profession." (p. 1910)

1068 "A rationale of the Law of Homicide,"
      by Wechsler and Michael. COLUMBIA
      LAW REVIEW. 37, 1937.

1069 "Resuscitation and euthanasia," by B. P.
      Galbally. THE AUSTRALIAN NURSE'S
      JOURNAL. 2:26-29, June, 1973.
      Medical science now has the ability
      to technologically create an artificial
      survival. The physician is expected to
      carry on resuscitation as long as brain
      death remains unproven. In treating
      the patient, distinctions are made
      between acts of omission and commission;
      between deliberate actions and crimes of
      omission. Distinctions are made between
      active and passive behavior. Galbally
      also discusses the legal implications
      of terminating resuscitative measures.

1070 "Right to die," CALIFORNIA WESTERN LAW
      REVIEW. 10:613-617, Spring, 1974.

1071 "Right to die," HOUSTON LAW REVIEW.
      7:654, May, 1970.

1072   "Right to die,"   by D. Gould. NEW STATES-
          MAN. 77:402, March 21, 1969.
          Suggests that society would have to
       re-define its views concerning the
       tragedy of death with the arrival of
       the British Voluntary Euthanasia Bill.
       The bill was sponsored by the Euthanasia
       Society of London and by Lord Reglan.

1073   "Right to die - a debate," by A. L.
          Wolbarst. FORUM. 94:330-334, December,
          1935.
          Covers various aspects of the legal
       questions which arise when euthanasia
       is considered. The article presents
       a discussion about euthanasia in relation
       to the incurably ill, the imbecile,
       and the insane.

1074   "Right to die with dignity," MEDICAL WORLD
          NEWS. 10:20, February 21, 1969.
          Dr. Walter Sackett, a representative
       in the Florida Legislature, is a pro-
       ponent of euthanasia. His views and
       legislative progress concerning eutha-
       nasia are reported.

1075   "The right to kill - continued," TIME.
          26:39-40, November 25, 1935.
          Miss Anna Becker, 34, was badly in-
       jured in an automobile crash. Her body
       has never been able to fully recover.
       She is constantly in pain. In a letter
       which she wrote to a physician, Miss
       Becker made a plea for her life to be
       ended. Legal opinions and analogies to
       the American Psychology ensued.

1076   "Shall we legalize hommcide?" OUTLOOK..
          82:252-253, February 3, 1906.
          In 1906, a bill was brought before
       the Ohio Legislature recommending
       the legalization of euthanasia. Moral
       and ethical arguments are raised

1077 "Should we legalize mercy killing" by H.
A. Davidson. MEDICAL ECONOMICS.
27(8):64-66, passim, May, 1950.

1078 "Shall we legalize mercy killing? - pro
and con," READER'S DIGEST. 33:94-98,
November, 1938.
Discusses the pros and cons of the
legalization of euthanasia.

1079 "Some non-religious views against proposed mercy killing legislation," by
Yale Komisar. MINNESOTA LAW REVIEW.
42:969-1042, May, 1958.
Raises objections to the legalization
of voluntary euthanasia. For related
information see: Williams. MINNESOTA
LAW REVIEW, November, 1958.

1080 "Study of two crimes," by R. Piedelievre.
ANNALES DE MEDECINE LEGALE. (Paris)
40:364-365, July-August, 1960. (French)

1081 "Suicide, euthanasia and the law," by G.
A. Friedman. MEDICAL TIMES. 85(6):681-
689, June, 1957.
Discusses the criminal action implied
by suicide and analyzes the idea of
euthanasia in the light of the Roberts
case, Repouille vs U. S., State versus
Sander; Paight and Mohr cases. These
cases involved the active euthanasia of
terminally ill patients.

1082 "Suspected natural deaths; medicolegal
study," by B. El Din. ANNALES DE
MEDECINE LEGALE DE CRIMINOLOGIE ET DE
POLICE SCIENTIFIQUE, MEDECINE SOCIALE,
ET TOXICOLOGIE. 20:121-158, March-
April, 1940.

1083   "Termination of life," BRITISH MEDICAL
       JOURNAL. 1:187-188, January 23, 1971.
          Voicing opposition to euthanasia
       legislation, the writer reveals the
       oppression rather than civil liberty
       that results from a voluntary euthanasia
       bill.

1084   "To be or not to be: voluntary eutha-
       nasia bill," NURSING TIMES. 65:382,
       March 20, 1969.
          The purpose of the Voluntary Euthanasia
       Bill is to authorize physicians to
       practice euthanasia on patients with
       irremediable conditions, providing
       that particular patients have signed a
       declaration requesting euthanasia not
       less than thirty days before enactment.
       The eight clauses that must be signed
       by the patient requesting euthanasia
       are discussed briefly.

1085   "Unusual case of murder of husband by
       wife during early stages of general
       paralysis; expert testimony and medico-
       legal considerations concerning case
       after malarial therapy," by G. Volpi-
       Ghirardini. RASSEGNA DI STUDI PSICYIAT-
       RICI. 29:297-315, March-June, 1940.
       (Italian)

1086   "The verdict in the Lille trial." SEMANE
       DES HOPITAUX: INFORMATIONS (Supplement
       to SEMAINE DES HOPITAUX DE PARIS. 41:
       4-5, October 30, 1962. (French)

1087   "Vexing problems in forensic medicine,"
       by Phillips Frohman. NEW YORK
       UNIVERSITY LAW REVIEW. 31:1215-1222,
       1956.
          Raises some objections to the American
       Euthanasia Bill and questions the true
       mercy of euthanasia.

1088 "Voluntary euthanasia," AMERICAN JOURNAL
OF PUBLIC HEALTH AND NATION'S HEALTH.
22:180-182, February, 1932.
An editorial delivered by Dr. Millard
to the Society of Medical Officers in
England. Advocates the legalization
of voluntary euthanasia and outlines
essential provisions of such an act.

1089 "Voluntary euthanasia," by W. G. Earengey.
MEDICO-LEGAL AND CRIMINOLOGICAL REVIEW.
8:91-110, April, 1940.
The legality of euthanasia as it affects
the doctor is examined by Judge Earengey. The Euthanasia Bill of the House
of Lords is analyzed. This bill is
opposed by many religious, social, and
medical leaders.

1090 "Voluntary euthanasia," by A. A. Moeres.
WASHINGTON LAW REVIEW. 45:239, April,
1970.

1091 "Voluntary mercy deaths: socio-legal
aspects of euthanasia," by A. A.
Levisohn. JOURNAL OF FORENSIC MED-
ICINE. 8:57, April-June, 1961.

1092 "Who signed for euthanasia," by F.
Anderson. AMERICA. 96:73, February,
1957.
A furore developed around a petition
submitted to the New Jersey Legislature bearing the signatures of 166
physicians. A newspaper, The Advocate,
published the petition in full with all
signatures. The resulting action
was chaotic, with many of the physicians
denying that they had ever signed such
a petition.

NEWSPAPER ARTICLES

1093 "British Government rejects Lords move
to legalize euthanasia," NEW YORK
TIMES. 5:5, November 29, 1950.

1094 "British House of Lords passes without
debate bill to allow doctors to end
lives of incurable patients who request
it," NEW YORK TIMES. 23:1, March 8,
1969.

1095 "Btitish Royal Commission opposes exempting
slayers from death penalty," NEW YORK
TIMES. 35:2, September 24, 1953.

1096 "C. E. Nixdorf, Euthanasia Society of America, proposes NEW YORK STATE bill for
legalization," NEW YORK TIMES. 21:7,
January 27, 1939.

1097 "Cardinal Spellman backs World Medical
Association legislative council against
euthanasia," NEW YORK TIMES. 38:5,
May 8, 1950.

1098 "Dr. Jahoda urges legalization," NEW
YORK TIMES. 3:7, June 28, 1956.

1099 "E. H. Levine recommends judges be em-
powered to appoint committee to study
advisability of specific mercy killing,"
NEW YORK TIMES. 20:2, January 31,
1950.

1100 "Eugenics legislation and mercy killings
debated; concensus holds man not
ready to play God," NEW YORK TIMES.
28:2, November 16, 1962.

1101 "Euthanasia bill to be discussed in House
of Lords; wide attention given it in
press; clergy divided on bill; summary

NEWSPAPER ARTICLES

of provisions," NEW YORK TIMES.
22:4, November 11, 1936.

1102 "Euthanasia Society of America urges passage of proposed New York State bill,"
NEW YORK TIMES. 23:7, May 23, 1941.

1103 "Group of doctors, testifying at hearings on 'Death with dignity' ... disagree on whether terminally ill or
injured patients have a right to euthanasia," NEW YORK TIMES. 15:1, August
8, 1972.

1104 "Held on homicide and Sullivan's Law
charges," NEW YORK TIMES. 21:2,
October 14, 1939.

1105 "House of Lords votes down euthanasia
bill; Lord Dawson of Penn and Arch-
bishop of Canterbury urge against
bill," NEW YORK TIMES. 29:2, December
2, 1936.

1106 "Lord Ponsonby introduces bill in Parliament
to legalize euthanasia," NEW YORK TIMES.
29:7, November 5, 1936.

1107 "National Society for Legalization of
Euthanasia formed in United States;
Dr. F. C. Potter, president, on program," NEW YORK TIMES. 21:8, January
17, 1938.

1108 "New York State Senator Santangelo and
Assemblyman Cioffi offer bill against
mercy killing," NEW YORK TIMES. 9:2,
January 11, 1950.

1109 "New York State Senator W. E. Conrad and
Assemblyman W. C. Clancey offer bill

NEWSPAPER ARTICLES

to require doctors believing in mercy killing to state so on prescription blanks, calling cards and signs in offices," NEW YORK TIMES. 24:3, February 23, 1950.

1110 "Petition signed by 1,000 doctors asking legalization of voluntary euthanasia sent to New York State Legislature members," NEW YORK TIMES. 30:3, December 15, 1947.

1111 "Prevent issue from reaching floor at conference (American Academy of General Practice)," NEW YORK TIMES. 50:7, February 22, 1950.

1112 "Resolution adopted," NEW YORK TIMES. 58:4, November 28, 1948.

1113 "Resolution urging New York State Legislatureto ban approval offered, American Physicians Association and New York State Naturopathic Association Convention," NEW YORK TIMES. 9:5, November 27, 1948.

1116 "Senator J. H. Comstock introduces bill to legalize practice of euthanasia in Nebraska," NEW YORK TIMES. 7:1, February 3, 1937.

1115 "Senator Mahoney scores proposal," NEW YORK TIMES. 15:5, January 7, 1949.

1116 "Voluntary Euthanasia Society of London holds first public meeting; outline of bill to be introduced into Parliament," NEW YORK TIMES. 16:4, December 11, 1935.

THE LAW AND EUTHANASIA

SEE ALSO:
CASES OF MERCY KILLINGS

LIVING WILL

1117 "Christian affirmation of life," by Kevin
       D. O'Rourke. HOSPITAL PROGRESS. 55:
       65-67, July, 1974.
          Designed to meet the needs of
       Christians who wish to sign a "living
       will". The document expresses the
       truths of Christian faith and treats
       death as the last human act leading
       to eternal life.

1118 "Death with dignity; the debate goes on,"
       SCIENCE NEWS. 102:118, August 19,
       1972.
          Walter Sackett introduced a bill into
       the Florida Legislature concerning
       death with dignity. The living will
       document's terms of consent are dis-
       closed.

1119 "Due process of euthanasia: the living
       will - a proposal," by L. Kutner.
       INDIANA LAW JOURNAL. 44:539, Summer,
       1969.

1120 "Euthanasia is an act of love," by P.
       Torrissi. SEVENTEEN. 33:116, August,
       1974.
          Believes that when the practice of
       keeping the dying patient alive con-
       tributes to the prolonged suffering
       and overwhelming emotional and financial
       burdens on the family, the saving of
       that life can no longer be considered
       a gain   The Living Will document is
       discussed.

1121 "Living will - and the will to live,"
        by D. Dempsey. NEW YORK TIMES
        MAGAZINE. 12-13, passim, June 23,
        1974.
           David Dempsey reveals the many short-
        comings of living wills and examines
        the phrase of "the right to death with
        dignity". Before a verdict can be
        rendered on living will decisions, the
        four crucial aspects that should be
        reviewed are listed and discussed.

1122 "Living will; excerpts from last rights,"
        by M. Mannes. ATLANTIC MONTHLY.
        233:62-63, January, 1974.

1123 "The quality of death - editorial,"
        WORLD MEDICAL JOURNAL. 21:61-62,
        July-August, 1974.
           Summarizes the various views on
        euthanasia that were presented by
        members of the Third World Congress
        on Medical Law held in Gent. A
        copy of the living will document is
        included.

1124 "Right to die," by G. P. Thompson, et al.
        LANCET. 2:1037, November 14, 1970.
           G. P. Thompson suggests that a non-
        statutory declaration of wishes by a
        patient on file with his physician
        could avoid many of the conflicts
        which might arise in a voluntary eutha-
        nasia decision.

1125 "Right to die: living will prepared by
        Euthanasia Educational Fund of New
        York," JOURNAL OF THE KANSAS MEDICAL
        SOCIETY. 73:13, August, 1972.
           Reprints and describes the Euthanasia
        Society's Living Will document.

LIVING WILL

1126   "Right to die: will states patient's
      wishes," ALASKA MEDICINE. 14:67,
      July, 1972.
        Supplies a form for a letter of
      instruction which can be used by patients
      and given to the attending physician.
      This letter states the patient's wishes
      when decisions concerning his illness
      arise in the future.

1127   "A will to live," by W. Modell. NEW
      ENGLAND JOURNAL OF MEDICINE. 290:
      907-908, April 18, 1974.
        Dr. Modell released a copy of a person-
      al directive from an unidentified patient
      in order that others may use this
      recital of choices as a guide for
      patient's wishes concerning possible
      physician's actions when the patient
      could not make those wishes known.

NEWSPAPER ARTICLE

1128   "Ellen Levine letter on David Dempsey's
      June 23 article on "Living will" says
      equally important as right to die is
      right to know when one is dying," NEW
      YORK TIMES. VI. p. 2, July 21,
      1974.

THE MORALITY OF EUTHANASIA

1129   "About questioning the right to die:
      reprise and dialogue," by B. Armiger.
      NURSING OUTLOOK. 16:26-28, October,
      1968.
        Responds to a preceding article by
      Mrs. Shepard and questions the theo-
      logical validity of the "right to die".
      Sister Armiger argues that medical
      staff should exhaust the field of
      possible treatment in order to assist

life in the last years of patients.
Sister Armiger sees death as a ful-
fillment of life rather than extinction.

SEE ALSO: "This I believe ... about
questioning the right to die," by M.
W. Shepard. NURSING OUTLOOK. 16:22-
25, October, 1968.

1130 "Advising radical surgery: a problem in
medical morality," by J. C. Ford and
J. E. Drew. JOURNAL OF THE AMERICAN
MEDICAL ASSOCIATION. 151:711-716,
February 28, 1953.

1131 "Catholic theologian (Reverend Gerald
Kelly) defends man's right to die,"
JOURNAL OF THE AMERICAN MEDICAL
ASSOCIATION. 180:23-24 (Adv), April,
28, 1962.
A Roman Catholic priest discusses
euthanasia primarily from the materialis-
tic viewpoint. What will a prolonged-
terminal illness do to the working-man's
hard-earned life savings? Active euthanasia is not recommended. Several passive
forms, while not termed euthanasia, are
discussed.

1132 "Chaplain and the dying patient," by J.
R. Cavanagh. HOSPITAL PROGRESS. 52:
35-40, November, 1971.
Discusses the two relationships
between chaplain and dying patient -
the ethical and the pastoral. Definitions
of terms in the article prove very
helpful: reversible and irreversible
illness, the dying process, the act
of dying and death agony. Natural,
ordinary, and extraordinary means of
prolonging life are discussed. A
definition of suicide and murder is

included. Also included in this
article is a survey of student nurses'
reactions to the dying patient.

1133 "Christians and euthanasia," by S.S.B.
Gilder. CANADIAN MEDICAL ASSOCIATION
JOURNAL. 108:141, January 20, 1973.
   Two documents, a report of the General
Synod of the Dutch Reformed Church,
and an English work by Duncan Vere
are used to supply information on the
Christian viewpoints toward eutha-
nasia.

1134 "Coup de grace," by M. M. Shideler.
CHRISTIAN CENTURY. 83:1499-1502,
December 7, 1966.
   Emphasis is on the need to confer
"exercise freedom" by examining the
problems in the light of Christian
doctrine, making a responsible decision
and to act on it.

1135 "Coup de grace and the complexity of
decision," by J. B. Wilson. CHRISTIAN
CENTURY. 84:82-83, January 18, 1967.
   A critical assessment of M. M.
Shideler's "Coup de grace" article.

   See Also: "Coup de grace," by M. M.
Shideler. CHRISTIAN CENTURY. 83:
1499-1502, December 7, 1966.

1136 "Death by chance, death by choice; adaptation of death by choice," by D. C.
Maguire. ATLANTIC MONTHLY. 233:56-
65, June, 1974.
   "Medicine marches on. The law and
ethics straggle behind. We have the
knowledge to prolong life. Here, a
Catholic theologian asks if we have
the wisdom to end it." (P. 57)

1137　"The duty of using artificial means to preserve life,"　THEOLOGICAL STUDIES. 11:203, June, 1950.

1138　"The duty to preserve life,"　by G. Kelly. THEOLOGICAL STUDIES.　12:550, December, 1951.

1139　"A eutanasia,"　by H. R. de Almeida. BRASIL-MEDICO.　69(27-31):383-385, July 2-30, 1955.
　　　Approaches euthanasia from the Catholic viewpoint and presents arguments concerning the legalization of euthanasia.

1140　"Euthanasia,"　by A. V. Serra.　JORNAL DO MEDICO.　(Porto)　21(59):38-48, January 3, 1953.　(Spanish)
　　　Ponders most aspects of the subject, citing cases and presenting the Catholic viewpoint.

1141　"Euthanasia and death,"　by Reverend G. Gariepy.　CATHOLIC HOSPITAL. (Candad) 2:131-133, March-April, 1974.
　　　"The purpose of this analysis is to examine euthanasia and death, their implications, the guidelines taught by the Roman Catholic Church in relation to these issues, and the practical problems which are encountered by a patient, families and various health professionals ..." (p. 131)

1142　"Euthanasia and modern morality,"　by T. O. Martin.　THE JURIST.　10:437-464, October, 1950.

1143　"Euthanasia:　is merciful release wrong?" READER'S DIGEST.　52:105-107, June, 1948.

1144   "Euthanasia; moral aspects,"   by H. R.
       Werts. LINACRE QUARTERLY. 14(2):27-
       33, April, 1947.
       Condemns mercy killing in any form;
       discusses the moral and legal rights
       to life and argues against the state's
       right to deny life to deformed infants,
       the terminally ill, or social misfits.

1145   "The fight to live and the right to die,"
       by R. I. Gannon. AORN JOURNAL. 6:
       49-52, September, 1967.
       The beginning of the article presents
       a discussion on the constitution and
       American ethic. Emphasis is placed on
       the moral issues of euthanasia.

1146   "The human person: experimental laboratory
       or priviledged sanctuary," by Reverend
       Charles Carroll. HOSPITAL PROGRESS.
       52:35-41, June, 1971.
       After discussing liberalized abortion
       laws, the author presses for the main-
       tenance of a general quality of existence
       rather than a mere extenuation of a
       life-time. Theological expressions of
       euthanasia are related as the Papal
       comments are reviewed.

1147   "Jewish attitudes toward euthanasia,"   by
       F. Rosner. NEW YORK STATE JOURNAL
       OF MEDICINE. 67:2499-2506, September
       15, 1967.
       After a discussion of terminology
       and a presentation of some definitions,
       a brief introduction to euthanasia
       societies and some reasons for such
       societies' existence, the author
       launches into a discussion of the legal
       attitude toward euthanasia. In addition
       to defining and explaining the Jewish
       attitude toward euthanasia, the pros and
       cons, and protestant and catholic

attitudes are examined. Excellent
bibliography at the end of the article.

1148 "Keeping the dying alive: moral problem
of mercy killing," AMERICA. 114:6,
January 1, 1966.

1149 "Let the hopelessly ill die?" U. S.
NEWS AND WORLD REPORT. 55:18, July 1,
1963.
A brief analysis of views expressed
by Bishop Fulton J. Sheen on mercy
killing and the employment of extraordinary means is presented. The official
position of the Roman Catholic Church
as of 1957 with regard to euthanasia
is stated.

1150 "Let the terminal patient die? Here's
where religious leaders stand,"
MEDICAL ECONOMICS. 41:68-69, May 18,
1964.

1151 "License to life," CHRISTIANITY TODAY.
18:22-23, July 26, 1974.
With the acceptance of legalized
abortion comes the warning - first forced
sterilization once each family has
reached the optimum of three children;
next acceptance of passive euthanasia;
then active ... This editorial calls
upon Christians to voice their opposition
to such measures.

1152 "Life and death of the law," by D. J.
Keefe. HOSPITAL PROGRESS. 53:64-74,
March, 1972.
Father Keefe, a lawyer and priest,
presents both theological and legislative arguments surrounding life, death,
and the law. He treats legal rationality and freedom; the Judeo-Christian
tension between rationality and freedom;

law in service of myth; the failure
of the Utopian rationalization of man;
the Constitutional alternative to Utopia;
the mutability of myth; the liturgy of
civil religion; a problem for theo-
logians (civil and otherwise); facing
the people; law - fallen and unfallen;
messianism - the alternative to Historical determinism; Sacramental law as
Christian witness; freedom, worship and
loyalty; Christian faith - the basis of
future hope; symbols of death and life;
and explores the duty of pacifism.

1153 "Medical aspects relating to euthanasia,"
by L. Krause. MARYLAND STATE MEDICAL
JOURNAL. 2(3):131-136, March, 1953.
Dr. Krause draws from his personal
experience with his patients. He
questions christian argument for the
purpose of pain. Draws heavily from
the Bible. Asserts that he is "un-
hesitatingly a very positive champion
of the view that life should be preserved to its ultimate." (p. 133)

1154 "Medico-moral notes," by G. Kelly.
LINACRE QUARTERLY. 17(4):3-17,
November, 1951

1155 "Merciful or sinful," by M. G. Miro.
AMERICA'S. 10:37-38, April, 1958.

1156 "Mercy and Mr. Blanshard - reprint,"
COMMONWEAL. 71:144, October 30,
1959.
Appears as a reprint of an article
entitled: "The quality of mercy"
which is primarily a review of Paul
Blanshard's book American Freedom and
Catholic Power.

See Also: COMMONWEAL. 51:380-381,
January 13, 1950.

1157 "Moral consideration of prolonging life,"
by P. S. Rhoads. JOURNAL OF THE SOUTH
CAROLINA MEDICAL ASSOCIATION. 64:422-
428, October, 1968.

1158 "The moral limits of reanimation," by V.
Vic-dupont. REVUE DE L'INFIRMIERE.
21:219-221, March, 1971. (French)

1159 "Moral medical aspects of congenital mal-
formations," by N. Pappalepore.
REVISTA DE PATHOLOGIA CLINICA. (Parma)
19:390-401, July, 1964. (Italian)

1160 "Morality of breath," by Reverend J.
Schaefer. JOURNAL OF PASTORAL CARE.
25:112-116, June, 1971.

1161 "Morality: today I killed my best
friend," TIME. 85:74, passim, April
23, 1965.

1162 "Non-finisher," ECONOMIST. 230:24, March
29, 1969.
    Asserts one major objection to Lord
Raglan's euthanasia bill - the Christian ethic.

1163 "One stigma that won't beat a dogma
AMERICA. 95:557, September 15, 1956.
    The dogma of sanctity of human life
because of the existence of a soul does
not impede scientific progress; instead,
it stimulates it. To short-cut the
problem of suffering by murder deprives
society of scientific progress in
the areas of terminal illness and
disease.

1164 "The patient's right to die - moral

aspects of euthanasia," by J. H.
McClanahan. MEMPHIS MEDICAL JOURNAL.
38:303-316, August, 1963.

1165 "The prolongation of life," by Pope Pius
XII. AMERICAN QUARTERLY OF PAPAL
DOCUMENTS. 4:393, 1958.

Also in: POPE SPEAKS. 4:393,398. (No. 4)
1958.

Also in: OSSERVATORE ROMANO. 393-398,
1957.

1166 "Quality of mercy," COMMONWEAL. 51:380-
381, January 13, 1950.
The article is basically a criticism
of Paul Blanshard's American Freedom
and Catholic Power, 1949. It presents
the human condition of the Catholic as
totally confused as to the answers to
the problems arising from a discussion
or confrontation with issues surrounding euthanasia.

1167 "Right to die," by Reverend T. J. O'Donnell.
AORN JOURNAL. 1:27-33, March-April,
1963.
A theologian discusses euthanasia,
ordinary and extraordinary measures, and
moral opinions concerning euthanasia.
Additionally, he presents an investigation of the subject by example and
proposed solutions.

1168 "Right to die - what shall the church say?"
by J. R. Nelson. BULLETIN OF THE
AMERICAN PROTESTANT HOSPITAL ASSOCIATION.
32:2-3, Summer, 1968.
When discussing the right to die,
eight basic questions confront the
public. These questions: (1) Is man's
life exclusively his own? (2) Does
any person have the right ... to cut

the life of another person? (3) Where
is the essential reality of human life
to be found? (4) What actually con-
stitutes death? (5) Are extreme pain
and physical suffering always evil?
(6) Is death always man's last enemy?
(7) What are the familial and social
implications to prolonging life? and
(8) And what of the Hippocratic oath?
Also discussed is the compassion and
constancy of the church.

1169 "Sacredness of life," by W. M. Abbott.
AMERICA. 108:326, March 9, 1963.
In a fifteen page pamphlet, Cardinal
Suenas devotes the bulk of his message
to confronting active euthanasia
activists. He contends that one dare
not be a judge on whom should live
or die because each life is sacred in
that all are part of the Mystical Body
of Christ.

1170 "The sanctity of life," by G. Boas.
MARYLAND STATE MEDICAL JOURNAL. 2(3):
128-131, March, 1953.
The history of the sanctity of life
and its present legal status are
reviewed. Mr. Boas draws from the Ten
Commandments (particularly the fifth
and sixth) showing some basis for arguments on the sanctity of life. Argues
that the state has the right to take
a life but the individual does not have
this same right.

1171 "Science, religion and moral judgments,"
by E. W. Barnes. NATURE. 166:455-
457, September 15, 1950.
Bishop Barnes discusses the possible
role of euthanasia as a solution to
some of our problems, such as its role
in capital offenses, in the eradication

of abnormal genes, and in overpopulation.

1172 "Thomas More, the mercy killer," CATHOLIC
WORLD. 169:3-4, April, 1949.
The Euthanasia Society of America,
in an effort to get a sanction for a
euthanasia bill in Albany, asserted that
the Catholic Church sanctioned the
practice since it was advocated by
Thomas More, a canonized saint. There
is some question as to whether More
was speaking of situations similar to
the Euthanasia Society's beliefs or
merely suggesting that humans be guided
by reason.

1173 "To die with dignity," by Aidan M. Carr.
CATHOLIC DIGEST. pp. 104-108, April,
1974.
Carr presents a very organized
definition of what death with dignity
means. He also "clears-up" some common
misconceptions that some individuals
have concerning the Catholic Church's
stand on the matter. (Condensed from:
Homiletic and Pastoral Review, November,
1973)

1174 "Unfinished debate," COMMONWEAL. 51:
619-621, March 24, 1950.
This article begins with an analysis
of the much-publicized case of Dr.
Hermann Sander. From this dialogue,
the editorialist launches into a discussion of the Catholic role in the
euthanasia question and expresses an
opinion as to the Catholic's role
in euthanasia conflicts.

NEWSPAPER ARTICLES

1175 "Assailed by Vatican newspaper, Osservatore
Romano," NEW YORK TIMES. 49:4, November
30, 1941.

THE MORALITY OF EUTHANASIA

NEWSPAPER ARTICLES

1176 "Bishop Sheen and Dr. Rynearson see no moral difficulty in letting hopelessly ill patient die," NEW YORK TIMES. 17:3, June, 17, 1963.

1177 "Cardinal Griffin warns British doctors against practice," NEW YORK TIMES. 2:2, July 2, 1948.

1178 "Catholic College Press Association opposed," NEW YORK TIMES. 5:1, February 19, 1939.

1179 "Catholic war veterans score proposal," NEW YORK TIMES. 25:5, December 17, 1947.

1180 "Condemned by National Catholic Women's Union," NEW YORK TIMES. 25:5, August 19, 1947.

1181 "Denounced by Catholic War Veterans - New York Chapter," NEW YORK TIMES. 2:4, November 24, 1947.

1182 "Euthanasia approved by Bishop of Birmingham, England," NEW YORK TIMES. 40:3, March 8, 1937.

1183 "Euthanasia attacked by Reverend I. Cox," NEW YORK TIMES. 15:3, May 24, 1937.

1184 "Euthanasia condemned by Catholic Daughters of America," NEW YORK TIMES. 4:7, February 27, 1938.

1185 "Euthanasia defended by Bishop Barnes," NEW YORK TIMES. 6:3, September 4, 1950.

1186 "Euthanasia opposed by Reverend E. R. Moore," NEW YORK TIMES. 12:1; January 6, 1936.

THE MORALITY OF EUTHANASIA

1187 "Euthanasia scored by Catholic Daughters
      of America, New York State court,"
      NEW YORK TIMES. 11:2, May 19, 1950.

1188 "German church leaders helped form secret
      public opinion against measures,"
      NEW YORK TIMES. 4:6, June 11, 1943.

1189 "Hefelmann charges Roman Catholic Church
      was willing to tolerate mass mercy kill-
      ings," NEW YORK TIMES. 9:4, April
      8, 1964.

1190 "Msgr. J. S. Middleton condemns mercy
      as murder," NEW YORK TIMES. 23:2,
      January 10, 1949.

1191 "Msgr. McCormick scores practice and
      American Euthanasia Society move to
      legalize it; refuses society president
      Reverend C. F. Potter's challenge to
      publically debate; Potter charges
      he misquotes New York State penal law,"
      NEW YORK TIMES. 28:3, December 9,
      1947.

1192 "Pope bars practice of euthanasia by
      Roman Catholic doctors as contributing
      to manifest law of God," NEW YORK
      TIMES. 3:5, September 12, 1956.

1193 "Pope Paul equates euthanasia with
      abortion and declares that Christian
      anthropology observes absolute respect
      for man from conception to death,"
      NEW YORK TIMES. 2:4, October 13,
      1970.

1194 "Pope Paul VI urges participants at
      International College of Surgeons
      Convention to help Roman Catholic Church
      defend Christian ethics," NEW YORK
      TIMES. 13:5, June 4, 1972.

1195 "Pope Pius gives allied doctors ruling,"
        NEW YORK TIMES. 10:4, January 31, 1945.

1196 "Pope Pius XII states Roman Catholic
        Church's position to Allied Medical
        Officers," NEW YORK TIMES. 4:1,
        February 14, 1945.

1197 "Pope reaffirms condemnation," NEW YORK
        TIMES. 20:5, November 25, 1957.

1198 "Pope reconfirms condemnation but approves
        relief of pain of dying even if life
        if thereby shortened," NEW YORK
        TIMES. 1:5, February 25, 1957.

1199 "Potter answers Mc Cormick in sermon,"
        NEW YORK TIMES. 35:6, December 16,
        1947.

1200 "Practice of euthanasia scorned by German
        Confessional Church," NEW YORK TIMES.
        4:3, August 4, 1944.

1201 "Practice for race improvement and economic
        reasons condemned by Roman Catholic
        Church," NEW YORK TIMES. 25:8, Decem-
        ber 6, 1940.

1202 "Practice opposed by Catholic Daughters
        of America," NEW YORK TIMES. 9:1,
        February 28, 1942.

1203 "Roman Catholic clerks scorn speech for
        mercy death ideas; priest refuses to
        offer invocation," NEW YORK TIMES.
        6:8, July 21, 1951.

1204 "Rabbi L. I. Newman opposes mercy killing,
        sermon," NEW YORK TIMES. 26:2, January
        22, 1950.

THE MORALITY OF EUTHANASIA

1205 "Religious and moral issue in prolongation
of life of dying patients as distinct
from mercy killings discussed," NEW
YORK TIMES. IV. 6:1, May 23, 1965.

1206 "Reverend Dr. McComb charges advocates
disregard religion," NEW YORK TIMES.
22:8, January 17, 1949.

1207 "Scored by Cardinal Griffin," NEW YORK
TIMES. 5:5, October 8, 1947.

1208 "379 Protestant and Jewish clergymen
ask New York State Legislature legal-
izing mercy killings," NEW YORK
TIMES. 25:3, January 6, 1949.

1209 "U. S. Presbyterian Church General Council
opposes legalization," NEW YORK TIMES.
22:2, May 24, 1951.

PEDIATRICS

1210 "Agonizing decision of Joanne and Roger
Pell," by T. Morse. READER'S DIGEST.
100:69-73, passim, February, 1972.
Condensed from: GOOD HOUSEKEEPING,
January, 1972.
    Whether or not to withhold treat-
ment from an infant with spina bifida
is a most difficult decision. Joanne
and Roger Pell's decision-making process
lends insight into a parent's attitudes
and emotions in reaching the decision
to withhold treatment.

1211 "Are premature babies worth saving?"
by G. Griffith. NURSING MIRROR AND
MIDWIVES JOURNAL. 110:1647-1648,
August 5, 1960.

1212 "A complex moral question facing doctors
and families is whether infants with
incurable birth defects should be
allowed to die," THE NATIONAL OB-
SERVER. 11/10-7, 1973.

1213 "Death of a son," by P. D. Sholin.
READER'S DIGEST. 94:141-144, January,
1969.
"There is no need to prolong life
beyond the point where the patient can
respond to his environment." (p. 141)
A minister-father discusses his
severely brain-damaged infant son and
the decision not to prolong his son's
hopeless life. Some suggestions on
euthanasia's legalization are analyzed.

1214 "A debate on euthanasia for malformed
children" SEMAINE DES HOPITAUX:
INFORMATIONS; supplement to: SEMAINE
DES HOPITAUX DE PARIS. 31:4-5 and
4-10, July, 1962. (French)

1215 "Delivery room dilemmas," by G. Kelly.
HOSPITAL PROGRESS. 36(3):58, March,
1955.

1216 "Doctors ask for guidelines for mongoloid children," CANADIAN DOCTOR.
50:20, January, 1973.
There exists no consensus of opinion
as to what is right in cases involving
the methods which either should or
should not be employed in treating
a mongoloid child. A plea is made
for effective guidelines which would
assist the physician in determining
what course of action should be taken.

1217 "Doctor's dilemma in Down's syndrome and
duodenal atresia," by J. G. Randolph.
HOSPITAL PHYSICIAN. 10:23, September,

1974.
Suggests that the participating
physician take a much more active role
in disclosing the full potentialities
of the employment of extraordinary
measures for infant deformities.

1218 "The dramatic trial at Liege and the
serious problems caused by thalidomide
and by euthanasia," JORNAL DO MEDICO.
(Porto) 50:46-50, January 5, 1963.
(Portuguese)
The mercy killing of a thalidomide
baby girl grossly deformed caused
much furor. The case as well as an
analysis of the thalidomide "problem"
is condensed in an interview reported
here with Professor Miller Guerra.

1219 "Drug that left a trail of heartbreak:
thalidomide," LIFE. 53:24-36, August
10, 1962.
A pictorial documentary of the trials
and heartbreaks caused by the infant-
deforming drug, thalidomide, is presented in a series of successive articles.
Individual cases of deformed infants,
Dr. Kelsey's fortitude in keeping the
drug off the U. S. markets, and the
shock of William S. Merrill Company are
a few of the subjects reported in this
issue.

1220 "Ethical and social aspects of treatment of spina bifida," by R. B.
Zachary. THE LANCET. 2:274-276,
August 3, 1968.
Three options open to babies born
with myelomenigocele are given. The
first two options are destructive to
the child. The third is planned treatment of the child so that the handi-
caps are minimal.

1221   "Ethical issues in biomedicine: choices
       on everyone's conscience,"   by R. J.
       Trotter.   SCIENCE NEWS. 100:275-276,
       October 23, 1971.
          Reviews the ethical issues involved
       in the determination of a course of
       treatment to be employed when faced
       with the decision to treat or not to
       treat a mongoloid infant.

1222   "Euthanasia in children,"   by W. H. Wolters.
       MAANDSCHRIFT VOOR KINDERGENEESKUNDE.
       (Leiden)   39:177-188, August, 1972.
       (Dutch)

1223   "Euthanasia: should one kill a child in
       mercy?"   by R. Oulahan, Jr.   LIFE.
       53:34-35, August 10, 1962.
          A storm of controversy surrounds the
       mercy killing of deformed infants by
       their mothers.   Public opinion polls
       are cited, and theological and par-
       liamentarian views are disclosed.

1224   "Fortune survey: mercy killings," FORTUNE.
       16:106, July, 1937.
          Analyzes social attitudes toward the
       defective infant and incurably ill
       with specific regard to mercy killing.
       In this survey, a slight majority
       favored euthanasia of defective infants
       under certain circumstances.

1225   "God committee: life-death decision
       concerning infants suffering from
       meningomyelocele,"   by E. Freeman.
       NEW YORK TIMES MAGAZINE.   84-86,
       passim, May 21, 1972.

1226   "God squad: life should be safeguarded,"
       by Joseph L. Lennon.   RHODE ISLAND
       MEDICAL JOURNAL.   47:334-337, August,
       1974.

Discusses the medical dilemmas which society must currently face, such as the prolongation of lives of the retarded and infants with birth defects, and the length of time which the dying patient's life should be sustained. The right to life, the obligation to sustain life, and passive euthanasia are discussed.

1227 "Goodbye; how G. R. Long killed his daughter," TIME. 48:32, December 2, 1946.
G. R. Long put to a merciful death his seven-year-old deformed, imbecile daughter. The act and the events surrounding the act are reported.

1228 "Hardest choice: life or death for grossly malformed infants," TIME. 103:84, March 25, 1974.
One of the hardest choices parents of deformed babies must face is whether or not treatment, which merely prolongs the child's life at a level classed somewhat less than human, should continue. Cases are cited and noted authorities interviewed.

1229 "Histologic studies on lungs of newborn in medicolegal determination of infanticide," by N. Masaki and K. Fujii. JAPANESE JOURNAL OF MEDICAL SCIENCES, 7, 1940.

Also in: SOCIAL MEDICINE AND HYGIENE. 3:198-199, December, 1940

1230 "Infanticide," by J. C. M. Matheson. MEDICO-LEGAL AND CRIMINOLOGICAL REVIEW. 9:135-152, July, 1941.
Reviews medical questions involving infanticide; presents statistics

(including abortion) and discusses
the histories of several infanticide
cases.

1231 "Infanticide - medico-legal aspects,"
by G. M. Davidson. JOURNAL OF
CRIMINAL PSYCHOPATHOLOGY. 2:500-511,
April, 1941.

1232 "Infanticide - who makes the decision?"
by B. Gimbel. WISCONSIN MEDICAL
JOURNAL. (Madison) 73:10-11, May,
1974.
    Two court cases involving the per-
formance of surgery on deformed babies
ask the title question, yet receive
different answers. Barry Gimbel believes
that the ultimate decision should be
in the hands of the parents whose life
is most directly affected by the deformed infant.

1233 "Is there a right to die - quickly?" by
J. M. Freeman. JOURNAL OF PEDIATRICS.
80:904-905, May, 1972.
    Dr. Freeman asks, "if in those rare
instances in pediatrics where heroic
measures are avoided, should society
not allow physicians to hasten the
inevitable course?"

    See Also: "Whose suffering?" by R.
E. Cooke. JOURNAL OF PEDIATRICS.
80:906-907, May, 1972.

1234 "Lesson of Liege: Van de Put baby,"
AMERICA. 107:1239, December 15, 1962.
    Suzanne Van de Put took the life of
her deformed infant daughter. The case
and Mrs. Van de Put's subsequent trial
and acquittal are briefly discussed.

PEDIATRICS

1235   "Let the blighted babies die - or not,"
       MEDICAL WORLD NEWS. 13:27-28, November
       17, 1972.
           Presents pro and con arguments on
       whether or not vigorous treatment
       should be withheld from infants with
       spina bifida. Reviews statistics
       accumulated by Dr. Lorber of Britain's
       Sheffield University Hospital and Dr.
       Freeman, of University of Pennsylvania,
       School of Medicine.

1236   "Letter: euthanasia and children: the
       injury of continued existence," by
       H. T. Englehardt, Jr. JOURNAL OF
       PEDIATRICS. 83:170-171, July, 1973.
           Places emphasis on maintenance of
       a quality of existence not merely pro-
       longing the duration of an individual's
       existenc--no matter what the indignity.

1237   "Mercy killer: legal and moral problems
       raised by acquittal in murder of thalid-
       omide infant," ECONOMIST. 205:643,
       November 17, 1962.
           The author uses the recent acquittal
       of Mme. Vandeput and others as a
       launching point for a discussion of
       euthanasia. Distinctions are made as
       well as a prediction of the extent to
       which British popular sentiment would
       affect future cases.

1238   "Mongoloids and morality," AMERICA.
       95:608, September 29, 1956.
           An argument to have the existence
       of mongolism removed as a crutch for
       euthanasia is presented. An assertion
       is made that a cure for mongolism is
       "just around the corner".

1239   "Murder for mercy's sake," by C. J.
       McNaspy. AMERICA. 107:1242-1244,

December 15, 1962.
Father McNaspy expounds on the in-
alienable right to life that infants
and all humans should enjoy. He warns
society about its growing permissiveness
towards infanticide and all forms of
mercy killings and sees it as a serious
threat to our humanitarianism.

1240 "My little girl is unhappy - case of
Suzanne Vandeput," NEWSWEEK. 60:62,
November 19, 1962.
Mrs. Vandeput, as an act of mercy,
caused the death of her thalidomide-
deformed infant daughter. The case is
reported.

1241 "Pediatric ethical question," by B. S.
Veeder. JOURNAL OF PEDIATRICS. 58:
604-605, April, 1961.
A pediatric problem, such as whether
or not corrective surgery should be
performed on a mongoloid child with
a cardiac lesion, is posed.

1242 "Playing God," AMERICA. 107:1118, November
24, 1962.
A critical analysis of the acquittal
of the family at Liege, Belgium ... a
distinction between abortion and euthanasia is mentioned.

1243 "Problem of social control of congenital
defective, education, sterilization,
and euthanasia," by F. Kennedy.
AMERICAN JOURNAL OF PSYCHIATRY. 99:
13-16, July, 1942.
Euthanasia for the ill should never
be legalized. However, euthanasia for
those hopeless ones who should never have
been born "nature's mistakes" is
staunchly supported. Once the defective
child has reached the age of five years,

upon the application of his guardian,
he should be examined by a board to
determine if euthanasia should be
applied.

1244 "Prolonging life. 4. Nurse's burden,
doctor's decision," by J. Pells.
NURSING TIMES. 70:393-394, March 14,
1974.
Jeanne Pells believes that nurses
must voice their thoughts when faced
with morally questionable situations.
However, she also believes that nurses
should be in possession of all the
available facts before they do any
condemning of the medical staff's
actions in these questionable cases.
A case of the third birth of a spina
bifida baby to a mother is one questionable situation which is examined by
Pells in this article.

1245 "Quality of mercy: mongoloid son,"
TIME. 76:64, July 11, 1960.
George E. Johnson took the life of
his thalidomide deformed son. A
report of the incident is presented.

1246 "Right to die - a father speaks," by
B. Bard, et al. ATLANTIC MONTHLY.
221:59-62, April, 1968.
Mr. Bard argues for the right of
the hopelessly mongoloid infant to
die. He cites the case of his son and
describes the events which surrounded
his, his wife's, and his son's very
short existence together. Mr. Bard
implies support for a form of euthanasia
in these cases, and he suggests that
the entire subject of euthanasia needs
to be reexamined.

1247 "The right to kill," by Gregg.
AMERICAN REVIEW. 237:239-242, 1934.
Gregg discusses an "almost common"
practice among physicians and midwives not to respirate "monstrous"
deformed babies.

1248 "The right to kill - continued," TIME.
26:37-38, passim, December 2, 1935.
Discusses the physician's right to
bring to a merciful death defective
newborn infants and suffering incurables.
Numerous case histories are used to
illustrate points made in this discussion.

1249 "Salvage," by R. M. Forrester. THE
LANCET. 1:262-263, January 30, 1965.
Dr. Forrester examines the factors
which should govern decisions concerning
the treatment of abnormal or mortally
ill children by relating the religious,
medical, and social problems he has
encountered in his pediatric practice
with these children.

1250 "Shall this child die?" NEWSWEEK. 82:
70, November 12, 1973.
Deliberate withholding of vital
treatment to forty-three hopelessly
ill or congenitally deformed infants
by Dr. Raymond Duff and Dr. A. G. M.
Campbell is discussed in an effort
to stimulate open debate. "The public
has got to decide what to do with
vegetable members who have no human
potential," states Dr. Duff.

1251 "Should doctors let deformed babies die?"
by A. J. Snider. SCIENCE DIGEST.
75:47-48, 55, February, 1974.
Suggests that medical science's curi-
osity can preclude its ethics. Snider

compares arguments for and against
maintaining the continued existence
of the deformed baby. Medical
research is contrasted with man's
humanity to man.

1252 "Thalidomide homicide," TIME. 80:67,
November 16, 1962.
Suzanne Van de Put drugged her
thalidomide baby daughter because
of her deformity. The case is reported.

1253 "The thalidomide tragedies," by E.
Aubertin. JOURNAL DE MEDECINE DE
BORDEAUX ET DU SUD-OUEST. 139:10001-
10003, September, 1962. (French)

1254 "Thoughts about euthanasia for malformed
newborns," by E. Picha. WIENER MED-
IZINISCHE WOCHENSCHRIFT. 114:779-780,
October 31, 1964. (German)

1255 "To save or let die - the dilemma of
modern medicine," by Richard A. Mc
Cormick, SJ. JOURNAL OF THE AMERICAN
MEDICAL ASSOCIATION. 229:172-176,
July 8, 1974.
Reflects on the medical dilemma
doctors and parents face when deformed
infants face treatment. Advocates
for guidelines that may help in
decisions about sustaining the lives
of grossly deformed and deprived infants.
States it is the task of the physician
to provide concrete categories or
presumptive biological symptoms for
this human judgment.

1256 "Tragedy at Leige: Van de Put's thalidomide baby," by J. Gallahue. LOOK.
27-72-74, March 12, 1963.
A detailed, thorough account of the
Van de Put trial for the mercy killing

of their deformed infant daughter.
Views of laymen, legal experts, and
the Catholic Church may be discerned
from this article.

1257 "Tragedy at Liege: Vandeput's thalidomide
baby - discussion," LOOK 27:16,
April 23, 1963.
Six letters supporting and condemning
the Vandeputs' action in the mercy
killing of their deformed infant daughter.
Some of the writers invoke the "wrath
of God" while others cry for a "sense
of decency" in these situations.

1258 "Tragic dilemma: life or death for
deformed infants - editorial," BRITISH
MEDICAL JOURNAL. 4:567, December 9,
1972.
The editorial tells of a case where
local authorities were called upon
to seek statutory powers whereby a
child would be given treatment to
which the parents object because they
know this treatment will not restore
the child to normal health, but,
nevertheless, save his life.

1259 "When should the patient be allowed to
die?" by Richard L. Peck. HOSPITAL
PHYSICIAN. 8:28-33, July, 1972.
A mongoloid infant with duodenal
atresia was allowed to starve to death.
Controversy arose. A study group
task force was formed at Johns Hopkins
Hospital to assist doctors when similar
situations arise again.

1260 "Who shall be the judge? Baby malformed
at birth, and choice of life or death
in doctor's hands," by F. Loomis.
READER'S DIGEST. 34:19-22, May,
1939.

Not every deformed human being is condemned to an unhappy, useless life. Dr. Loomis reports the case of an infant girl, born with only one leg (he delivered the child breech). Knowing the child's deformity, Dr. Loomis had to make the decision as to whether or not to slow the delivery and thereby allow the infant to die. Dr. Loomis chose to save the infant-girl's life and years later was to witness the happy results of this decision. This deformed individual had become a musician and a very productive member of society.

1261 "Whose suffering?" by Robert E. Cooke. JOURNAL OF PEDIATRICS. 80:906-907, May, 1972.
Dr. Robert Cooke repudiates the reasoning behind the passive euthanasia stand of Dr. J. Freeman and examines the aspects of Dr. Freeman's belief that infants have a right to die quickly.

SEE ALSO: "Is there a right to die - quickly?" by J. S. Freeman. JOURNAL OF PEDIATRICS. 80:904-905, May, 1972.

1262 "Whose suffering - editorial," JOURNAL OF PEDIATRICS. 80:907-908, May, 1972.
The editorial comment attempts to synchronize the ideas of Drs. Cooke and Freeman concerning euthanasia.

SEE ALSO: "Is there a right to die - quickly?" by J. S. Freeman. JOURNAL OF PEDIATRICS. 80:904-905, May, 1972

AND ALSO: "Whose suffering?" by Robert

E. Cooke. JOURNAL OF PEDIATRICS. 80: 906-907, May, 1972.

NEWSPAPER ARTICLES

1264 "E. Freeman article on ethics surrounding birth of child with meningomyclocele, severe deformity," NEW YORK TIMES. VI. p. 84, May 21, 1972.

1265 "Frederic Greenberg article discusses from perspective of justice and fairness; question of euthanasia for severely retarded or handicapped children; says central issue of justice is equal allocation of right to life of all children, even against the wishes of their parents and if necessary through judicial intervention," NEW YORK TIMES. 35:2, April 22, 1974.

1266 "Haisilden, Dr. Harry H. - editorial on his administering drug to relieve suffering of defective child though the act shortens its life," NEW YORK TIMES. 12:5, November 15, 1917.

1267 "J. P. Kennedy Jr. Foundation sponsors symposium on mental retardation, human rights and biomedical research at which recent cases of mongoloid baby who was allowed to starve to death," NEW YORK TIMES. 33:1, October 17, 1971.

1268 "Johns Hopkins Hospital symposium pre-views J. P. Kennedy Jr. Foundation film recounting case of birth of mongoloid," NEW YORK TIMES. 31:1, October 15, 1971.

PEDIATRICS

NEWSPAPER ARTICLES

1269 "Mother starts nine months sentence for
     killing three-year-old, defective son,"
     NEW YORK TIMES. 2:6, November 2,
     1964,

1270 "Mothers in drought-stricken Puno, Peru,
     kill newborn babies rather than see
     them die of hunger," NEW YORK TIMES.
     69:1, June 4, 1967.

1271 "Reverend Richard A. McCormick, Jesuit
     at Kennedy Center for Bioethics at
     Georgetown University says infants
     should be allowed to die when they
     are so seriously deformed that there
     is no hope for their having human
     relationships; article in AMA Journal;
     offers as a guideline in decisions
     about sustaining life 'potential for
     human relationships' associated
     with infants condition," (S). NEW
     YORK TIMES. 32:2, July 8, 1974.

1272 "Senate sub-committee hearings on right
     to survive hears testimony that several
     thousand mentally and physically de-
     fective babies are allowed to die
     each year when medical treatment is
     withheld; doctors say one factor in
     decision is inability of some parents
     to afford expensive medical care needed
     to maintain severely handicapped children;
     hearings were prompted by report that
     treatment of forty-three deformed babies
     at Yale-New Haven Hospital had been
     stopped because prognosis for meaning-
     ful life was poor, " (S). NEW YORK
     TIMES. IV. 7:3, June 16, 1974.

1273 "The attitudes of physicians toward
prolonging life," by Terry A. Travis,
Russell Noyes, Jr., and Dennis R.
Brightwell. INTERNATIONAL JOURNAL
OF PSYCHIARTY IN MEDICINE. 5(1):17-
26, 1974.
Reports the results of a brief
questionnaire concerning the care of
terminally ill patients which was
distributed to all physicians in the
State of Iowa. Suggests that nearly
50% of those physicians responding
to the questionnaire revealed that
they frequently omitted life-prolonging
procedures or medications in the case
of hopelessly ill, dying patients.

1274 "Death and doctors," by K. S. Jones.
MEDICAL JOURNAL OF AUSTRALIA. 49(2):
329-334, September 1, 1962.
Recommends euthanasia as a potential
treatment for the dying patient. Claims
that when death is almost immediate no
real problem in medical treatment exists.
However, when the dying patient's illness
causes the individual to linger, problems do arise. An analysis is presented concerning who initiates the
proceedings and by whom this decision
is made. Editorials appearing in
THE LANCET and NEW YORK ACADEMY OF
MEDICINE BULLETIN are discussed as well
as statistical information reviewed.

1275 "Doctors vote 75-66 for 'death with
dignity'," HOSPITAL ADMINISTRATION
IN CANADA. 16:7-8, August, 1974.

1276 "Euthanasia," JOURNAL OF THE AMERICAN
MEDICAL ASSOCIATION. 218:249, October
11, 1971.
Reports the results of a questionnaire
given to physicians, medical students,

and nurses concerning negative and positive euthanasia.

1277 "Euthanasia poll: Gallop," READER'S DIGEST. 104:113, February, 1974.
In the middle of 1973, a Gallop poll was taken in order to ascertain general public views on euthanasia. A comparison is made of the results of the 1973 poll and the results of a similar poll taken in 1950.

1278 "Euthanasia: should one kill a child in mercy," by R. Oulahan, Jr. LIFE. 53:34-35, August 10, 1962.
A storm of controversy surrounds the mercy killing of deformed infants by their mothers. Public opinion polls are cited, and theological and parliamentarian views are disclosed.

1279 "Fortune survey: mercy killings," FORTUNE. 16:106, July, 1937.
Analyzes social attitudes toward the defective infant and incurably ill, with specific regard to mercy killing. In this survey, a slight majority of those questioned favored euthanasia of defective infants under certain circumstances.

1280 "How do nurses feel about abortion and euthanasia," by N. K. Brown, et al. AMERICAN JOURNAL OF NURSING. 71: 1413-1416, July, 1971.
Through a survey it was determined that a higher proportion of nurses reveived requests for euthanasia. And paradoxically , those nurses who are farthest removed from day-to day close patient care are most in favor of a euthanasia policy.

1281   "Infanticide," by J. C. M. Matheson.
       MEDICO-LEGAL AND CRIMINOLOGICAL
       REVIEW. 9:135-152, July, 1941.
          Reviews medical questions involving
       infanticide; presents statistics
       (including abortion); and discusses
       the histories of several cases.

1282   "Keeping patients alive: who decides?
       Growing debates over medical ethics,"
       U. S. NEWS AND WORLD REPORT. 72:44-
       49, May 22, 1972.
          Presents a survey conducted by the
       staff of the U. S. NEWS AND WORLD
       REPORT on death, euthanasia, and
       extraordinary means of prolongation of
       life. Doctors, theologians, and pro-
       minent persons are interviewed.

1283   "Let blighted babies die, or not,"
       MEDICAL WORLD NEWS. 13:27-28, November
       17, 1972.
          Presents pro and con arguments on
       whether or not vigorous treatment for
       spina bifida infants should be with-
       held. Reviews the statistics accumu-
       lated by Dr. Lorber of Britain's Shef-
       field University Hospital and Dr. Free-
       man of the University of Pennsylvania
       School of Medicine.

1284   "Older persons look at death," by H. Feifel.
       GERIATRICS. 11:127-130, March, 1956.
          The purpose of this study is to present
       some data regarding the conscious atti-
       tudes of persons 65 years of age and
       older regarding death. The subjects con-
       sisted of 40 white males living at a
       Veterans Administration Domiciliary.
       Results are given on a percentage basis.

1285   "Preservation of life," by N. K. Brown,
          et al. JOURNAL OF THE AMERICAN MEDICAL

ASSOCIATION. 211:76-81, June 5, 1970.
A survey of physician's attitudes
was taken with regard to euthanasia,
and the results examined. A copy of
this survey-questionnaire is included,
as well as charts and graphs providing
statistical information. A breakdown
of physician's age and specialty are
given.

1286 "Problems created by medical progress:
what do you do for the aged - and when
do you stop doing," MEDICAL WORLD
NEWS. 13:42-55, April 7, 1972.
Medical science has been able to
increase life expectancies of women by
sixteen years and men by thirteen
years. Duke University conducted a
study of aging, some of its findings
are reported. Medical advances and
educational advances in the area of
skilled care for the elderly are needed,
and it is hoped that foresight will
be shown in these areas in the near
future.

1287 "Quarter's polls on euthanasia," PUBLIC
OPINION QUARTERLY. 14(2):375, 1950.
Measures national opinions concern-
ing the practice of euthanasia.
Additional breakdown of information
is provided by sex and age.

1288 "Questions, Gallop poll," TIME. 49:
74, June 30, 1947.
Gallop poll statistics in the United
States are presented. Public's views
concerning incurable illness treatment and doctor-patient-involvement
in the termination of life upon request
are reviewed.

1289 "Terminal illness in the aged," by Exton-

Smith. THE LANCET. August 3, 1961.
States that in a study of 220 patients
dying in a London geriatric hospital,
eleven continually expressed a wish
to die.

1290 "Time to live and a time to die - how
physicians feel about euthanasia,"
by B. Rice. PSYCHOLOGY TODAY. 8:
29-30, September, 1974.
Briefly reports the results of a
questionnaire sent to a random sample
of three-thousand physicians. The
overwhelming majority of doctors
(79%) expressed some belief in the
patient's right to have a say about
his own death.

1291 "Views of the aged on the timing of death,"
by C. E. Preston and R. H. Williams.
GERONTOLOGIST. 11:300-304, Winter,
1971. (Part I)
Veterans and nursing home subjects
were interviewed concerning their
preferences for negative and positive
euthanasia. Half rejected withholding
of life-sustaining or life-shortening
procedures; one-quarter rejected life-
shortening but favored omission of life-
sustaining measures; and one-third
favored death through either omission
or commission. The subjects' attitudes
are correlated with their general quality
of existence.

1292 "Views on euthanasia," by E. H. Law.
JOURNAL OF MEDICAL EDUCATION. 46:
540-542, June, 1971.
Reports differing opinions among
medical students and graduate physicians
on euthanasia. Opinions were obtained
through a survey taken in 1966 at the
University of Washington, School of
Medicine.

STATISTICS

1293 "When life is no longer life," by M.
Fishbein. MEDICAL WORLD NEWS. 15:
84, March 15, 1974.
Euthanasia raises medical, legal,
and moral questions that have been
endlessly debated by members of all
professions concerned with the
individual and his welfare. Cases
are reviewed, and statistics of
250 Chicago internists and surgeons
opinions with regard to the practice
of euthanasia presented.

NEWSPAPER ARTICLES

1294 "Gallop poll shows 46% for it (euthanasia)
in United States; 69% in Great Britain,"
NEW YORK TIMES. III, 4:1, April 23,
1939.

1295 "Survey by Medical Opinion Magazine
finds acceptance of euthanasia has
become widespread in the medical profession; finds that, on choosing how
to die, 79% of doctors agree totally
or in some circumstances that people
have the right to make their wishes
known before serious illness strikes
and, on terminal care, 82% would
practice forms of passive euthanasia
on members of families, 86% on themselves (S)," NEW YORK TIMES. IV.
7:2, June 16, 1974.

SUICIDE

1296 Aided suicide among eskimos," TIME.
54:40, September 19, 1949.
Aided suicide has long been the
practice among the eskimos. The
case reported involves the "mercy
killing" in the form of aided suicide

of a tuberculin woman of 45 by her
son. The subsequent murder trial of
the son and the verdict of that trial
are reported.

1297 "Deed of friendship: Mary Happer shot
      by friend," NEWSWEEK. 65:30, April 26,
      1965.
         Dorothy Butts witnessed the constant
      pain of her friend, Mary Happer. Miss
      Butts, as an act of mercy, ended Ms.
      Happer's suffering and then took her
      own life.

1298 "Euthanasia," by Glanville Williams.
      MEDICO-LEGAL JOURNAL. 41:14-34, 1973.
         Williams, a long-time supporter
      of the euthanasia movement, has long
      "ceased to believe that .. rational
      argument can convince those who
      approach (euthanasia) with a firm
      rejection." He has found most argu-
      ments against it too superficial to
      mention but does state that doctor's
      fear "is that any legislation would
      be hedged about by unacceptable con-
      ditions." However, Williams points
      out that the legalization of eutha-
      nasia might make some individuals aware
      that they have some self-determining
      rights. The concept of omissions is
      discussed in the light of malformed
      children. Medical treatment and the
      consent of the patient, the dangers of
      honesty, the right to commit suicide
      and when there is a right to prevent
      an act of suicide are also topics
      discussed. The rationale for assist-
      ing a suicide and the legal status of
      such an involvement are analyzed as
      well as the reasons involved in fail-
      ing to prevent a suicide.

1299 "Euthanasia: s study in comparative
        criminal law," UNIVERSITY OF
        PENNSYLVANIA LAW REVIEW. 103:350-
        389, December, 1954.
          Compares suicide and mercy killing
        with criminal law.

1300 "Legalized suicide," by William T. Hall.
        DELAWARE STATE MEDICAL JOURNAL. 40:
        50-51, February, 1968.
          Dr. Hall discussed the act of dying
        with elderly members of his own family
        and with many of his dying patients.
        He concludes that they would vote
        ten to one in favor of legalized suicide.

1301 "Letter to the editor," by C. C. Catt.
        FORUM. 94:324, December, 1935.
          Supports Mrs. Gilman's argument that
        suicide is the individual's inherent
        right. The letter was prompted by
        Gilman's "Right to die" article.

        SEE ALSO: "The right do die," by C.
        P. Gilman. FORUM. 94:297-300.

1302 "Mercy killing," NEW REPUBLIC. 127:6,
        January, 1950.
          Discusses assisted suicide and makes
        special reference to the Sander case.
        (A case involving the injection of
        40 cc of air into the veins of a terminal-
        ill cancer patient)

        SEE ALSO: CASES OF MERCY KILLINGS:
        SANDER.

1303 "The right to die," by Zona Gale.
        FORUM. 95:110-112, April, 1936.
          Argues against euthanasia and suicide.
        Asserts that euthanasia is the "twin
        brother" of suicide.

SUICIDE

1304   "Right to die," by C. P. Gilman. FORUM.
            94:297-300, November, 1935.
            A plea by Mrs. Gilman for a more
        enlightened attitude toward euthanasia
        and suicide. This article was pub-
        lished after Mrs. Gilman's suicide in
        August, 1935.

1305   "The right to die-II---dinner in Thessaly,"
            by Sherwood Anderson. FORUM. 95:40-
            41, January, 1936.
            Comes to the defense and praise of
        Charlotte Gilman's suicide. Discusses
        the "good life" not merely life and of
        man's basic right to end his own life
        if he so chooses.

            SEE ALSO: "The right to die," by C.
        P. Gilman. FORUM. 94:297-300, November,
        1935.

1306   "Suicide and euthanasia," by H. Trowell.
            BRITISH MEDICAL JOURNAL. 2:275, May 1,
            1971.
            Refence is made to Dr. D. L. Henderson
        Smith's views on euthanasia. Trowell
        tells of the necessity of an individual,
        who under prescribed conditions might
        wi h euthanasia, to discuss those wishes
        with close relatives or friends.

1307   "Suicide and euthanasia," by H. Trowell.
            BRITISH MEDICAL JOURNAL. 3:50, July3,
            1971.
            Exception is taken by H. Trowell
        to articles written supporting some
        forms of euthanasia. The articles
        of Drs. Henderson Smith and D. Hooker
        are discussed.

1308   "Suicide, euthanasia and the law," by G.
            A. Friedman. MEDICAL TIMES. 85(6):
            681-689, June, 1957.

SUICIDE

Discusses the criminal action implied
by suicide and analyzes the idea of
euthanasia in the light of the Roberts
case, Repouille vs United States, State
vs Sander; Mohr and Paight cases.
These cases involve the active euthanasia
of terminally ill patients.

TERMINAL PATIENT CARE

1309 "As life ebbs," by V. W. Kasley. AMERICAN
JOURNAL OF NURSING. 38:1191-1198,
November, 1938.
Kasley presents an excellent
treatise on the nursing care of the
dying. Information about feeding the
dying patient is given in detail.
over, not only are the physical comforts
of the dying patient discussed, but
also included is a discussion on the
art of attending the dying patient's
mental needs.

1310 "The attitudes of physicians toward prolonging life," by Terry A. Travis,
Russell Noyes, Jr. and Dennis R.
Brightwell. INTERNATIONAL JOURNAL OF
PSYCHIATRY IN MEDICINE. 5(1):17-26,
1974.
Reports the results of a brief
questionnaire concerning the care of
terminally ill patients which was distributed to all physicians in the
state of Iowa. Suggests that nearly
50% of those physicians responding
revealed that they frequently omitted
life-prolonging procedures or medications
in the care of dying patients.

1311 "Can doctors be deaf to those begging
to die?" by David Hacker. THE NATION-
AL OBSERVER. September 28, 1974, p. 10.

The physician's right to administer
treatment to a patient severely ill
is examined, along with the views of
Dr. Engelhardt. Englehardt asserts
that physicians must pay more attention to the consequences of treating
the patient.

1312 "Care of the patient with advanced malignant disease," ARIZONA MEDICINE.
19:179-187, August, 1962.
The subject of cancer patient care
is discussed by a Catholic bishop,
an internist, an orthopedist, a radiologist, a psychiatrist, an oncologist,
and a research clinician.

1313 "Common sense in the intensive care unit,"
by H. A. Patterson. BULLETIN OF THE
NEW YORK ACADEMY OF MEDICINE. 47:
1363-1364, November, 1971.
Efforts to continue and prolong a
hopeless and miserable existence are
senseless. An analysis of this problem is presented in relation to intensive care units.

1314 "Death and doctors," by K. S. Jones.
MEDICAL JOURNAL OF AUSTRALIA. 49(2):
329-334, September 1, 1962.
Recommends that euthanasia be considered as a potential treatment for
the dying patient. Also, an analysis
is presented concerning who initiates
such proceedings and by whom this
decision is made. Editorials appearing
in THE LANCET and BULLETIN OF THE NEW
YORK ACADEMY OF MEDICINE are discussed,
as well as statistical information
reviewed.

1315 "Dignity in death: the application and
withholding of interventive measures,"

by T. T. Jones. JOURNAL OF THE
LOUISIANA STATE MEDICAL ASSOCIATION.
113:180-183, May, 1961.
A plea for comfort and relief to the
dying - not euthanasia but "aganthanasia"
has been proposed by Dr. Jones. In
this article, Dr. Jones relates many
of his experiences with terminally
ill patients which offer some proof
to his belief that medical personnel
need early instruction in the art of
attending the dying.

1316 "Dying with dignity," by E. Kubler-Ross.
THE CANADIAN NURSE. 67:31-35, October,
1971.
Mrs. Elizabeth Kubler-Ross and her
students interviewed 500 dying patients
as a means of learning from the patient
about what it is like to die and what
needs to be done for the dying. She
discusses the stages most patients
undergo before final acceptance of
death. And she makes some necessary
suggestions for providing more comfort in the care of dying patients.

1317 "Euthanasia and the care of the dying,"
by S. Bok. BIOSCIENCE. 23:461-464,
August, 1973.
S. Bok begins by defining euthanasia from various sources; these
definitions reflect varied sample of
differences which prevail when such a
definition is attempted. Legal proposals (with cases cited), and analyses
of the growing concern over dying,
dilemmas of the physician, including
treatment and/or lack of treatment;
and patient care are examined. Also,
Bok reflects on social norms.

1318   "Euthanasia: the care of the dying,"
         R. B. Robins. JOURNAL OF THE
         ARKANSAS MEDICAL SOCIETY. 66:277,
         January, 1970.
            Launches into a discussion of the
         idea of prolonging life and prolonging
         the act of dying. Patients' needs are
         considered. And the question: What
         would the doctor himself want if he
         were in the patient's condition? is
         posed.

1319   "Medical euthanasia: thesis," by C. F.
         H. Marx. JOURNAL OF THE HISTORY OF
         MEDICINE AND ALLIED SCIENCES. 7:403-
         416, 1952. (Translated from the
         original latin, 1826 by Walter Crane.)
            Reviews an alternative plan to mercy
         killing. Instead, four points by which
         a doctor's efforts to assist in a
         peaceful death are discussed: first,
         that by all means available, alleviate
         the patient's suffering through fore-
         sight and guidance; second, avoid
         and remove anything that might increase
         the patient's pain; third, cheer the
         patient's mind and body with con-
         vincing comforts and skilled nursing;
         and fourth, consideration of all persons
         or objects that such care enhances.
         The four types of patients' tempera-
         ments, and the various stages of
         physical death are additional subjects
         analyzed in detail in this excellent
         treatise on euthanasia.

1320   "Our service to the dying," by J. C.
         Doane. AMERICAN JOURNAL OF NURSING.
         38:1189-1190, November, 1938.
            The attention that medical personnel
         should render to dying patients and
         their families is spelled out nicely
         in this article.

1321   "Phantasies of the dying, some remarks
       on the management of death," by J.
       N. Glaister. THE LANCET. 2:315,
       August 6, 1921.

1322   "Philosophic implications of terminal
       illness," by James A. Knight.
       NORTH CAROLINA MEDICAL JOURNAL. 22:
       493-495, October, 1961.
         The problem of caring for the
       terminally ill patient by the physician
       involves more than adherence to strict
       medical practices. This idea is examined
       and the doctor's oblication and/or
       relationship to his patient is explain-
       ed.

1323   "Physician's attitudes toward the treat-
       ment of critically ill patients," by
       Diane Crane. BIOSCIENCE. 23:471-
       474, August, 1973.
         Physicians face unique problems when
       involved in a situation where eutha-
       nasia proves a possible alternative.
       Examined here are physician's feelings
       and attitudes. Problems as well are
       compared and contrasted from the legal
       approach.

1324   "Plea for eu'thanatos," by R. G. Twyn-
       cross. WORLD MEDICAL JOURNAL. 21:
       66-69, July-August, 1974.
         Argues that in considering euthanasia,
       one should only argue as a physician
       concerned chiefly in providing op-
       timum terminal care. Moreover, Dr.
       Twyncross asserts that he will not support
       a voluntary euthanasia plan, particularly
       when it appears to be based largely
       on confusion.

1325 "Problematical aspects of the phenomenon
of death," by H. P. Wasserman.
WORLD MEDICAL JOURNAL. 14:146-149,
September-October, 1967.
In this philosophical study of death,
Wasserman seeks to define the ideas
of life and death. Biologically, the
definition of death appears to be
related to irreversible loss of neural
function. Medical education pre-
pares the doctor for a realistic approach
to death. Wasserman recognizes that
death should be looked upon as an
inevitable end. Additionally, he
asserts that medical science should
develop a program of pre-mortem care
which provides euthanasia as a death
without suffering.

1326 "Procedures for the appropriate management of patients who may have supportive
measures withdrawn," by H. K. Beecher,
et al. JOURNAL OF THE AMERICAN MEDICAL
ASSOCIATION. 209:405, July 21, 1969.
Once extraordinary means are no longer
employed, a patient must be monitored
carefully and closely in order to
provide the maximum comfort available
and to provide an accurate death determination.

1327 "The right to live and the right to die,"
by A. G. Johnson. NURSING TIMES. 65:
575-577, May 13, 1971.
There exists three possible courses
of action one can take in the management
of terminally ill patients: prolong
life at all cost; terminate life by
deliberate positive action; or relieve
symptoms and allow nature to take its
course.

TERMINAL PATIENT CARE

1328   "Treatment of terminally ill patient
      discussed," AMA NEWS. 9:7, May 16,
      1966.
        The primary decision to prolong
      life in the care of a terminal illness
      belongs to the patient. In the case of
      the patient's inability to make the
      decision, the physician must use his
      judgment in conjunction with the
      patient's family and clergy.

NEWSPAPER ARTICLE

1329   "Article on Dr. Gary Leinbach, who while
      dying of cancer at age of 39, video-
      taped some major messages about care
      for the dying at University of Washington
      to be used as educational tool to
      select groups involved with dying
      patients," NEW YORK TIMES. 1:2, July
      22, 1974.

WAR CRIMES

1330   "Eugenic experiments conducted by Nazi's
      on human subjects," by C. P. Blacker.
      EUGENICS REVIEW. 44:9-19, April, 1952.
        Mass sterilization of human subjects
      and euthanasia for incurably insane
      and congenitally deformed infants are
      only a few of the atrocities which were
      perpetrated by the Nazis. Mr. Blacker
      tries to clarify the true meaning of
      "eugenics", which is often unjustly
      connected with the Nazi's racialist
      practices.

1331   "Euthanasia rejected by French Academy of
      Moral and Political Sciences.
      TODAY'S HEALTH. 28:65, April, 1950.
        The French Academy of Moral and
      Political Sciences has made a bold

rejection of any form of euthanasia.
Highlighted in the article is a recount
of recent experiences involving the
Nazi's death chamber.

1332 "Germany executes her unfit," by P. M.
    Straight. NEW REPUBLIC. 104:627-
    628, May 5, 1941.
        Reports the story of a mass mercy
    killing, views of the papacy, and the
    fate of two-hundred priests.

1333 "Mercy deaths in Germany; Gestapo's newest
    purge putting to death the mentally
    deficient," by W. L. Shirer. READER'S
    DIGEST. 38:55-58, June, 1941.
        Suspicion and mystery surround the
    deaths of the mentally ill in Germany.
    Hospital bombings, Gestapo cremations,
    and few details of death, lend to the
    mystery. Several theories as to the
    reasons for the mercy killings are
    discussed.

1334 "Nazi war crimes of a medical nature,"
    FEDERATION BULLETIN. 33:133, 142,
    1947.
        Discusses the Nazi view of euthanasia,
    namely, if it is right to take the life
    of useless and incurable persons, which
    as they point out has been suggested
    in England and in the United States,
    then it is right to take the lives of
    persons who are destined to die for
    political reasons.

1335 "Second Nuremberg Trial; report on Nazi
    medical experimentation (on euthanasia),"
    by C. Sillevaerta. BRUXELLES-MEDICAL.
    27:720-738, March 30, 1947.
        An examination, in French, of the
    war crimes divided into sections con-
    cerning "depositions concernant des
    mutilations et infections diverses;

despositions concernant l'execution du
programme d'euthanasie; and depot de
documents concernant l'euthanasie."

1336 "Swedish health board sanctions euthanasia
by MD," MEDICAL WORLD NEWS. 5:56-57, 60,
November 20, 1964.
A limited form of dodshjalp--death
help has been sanctioned by the Swedish
Board of Health. The specifics of the
dodshjalp situation are defined as well
as counter opposing views presented, including Dr. Alexander's analogy of World
War II mass murders in Germany.

1337 "Trials of war criminals before the Nuremberg Military Tribunal under Control Council Law No. 10, 1950," TESTI-
MONY AT THE NUREMBERG MEDICAL TRIAL,
1950.

NEWSPAPER ARTICLES

1338 "A. Klein terms mass murder of foreign
slave laborers. German mercy deaths,"
NEW YORK TIMES. 21:3, October 14, 1945.

1339 "Dr. W. Heyde sought 12 years for role in
Nazi euthanasia program surrenders," NEW
YORK TIMES. 5:6, November 13, 1959.

1340 "Dr. H. Pfannmueller gets 5 year sentence,
Munich, for part in Nazi program," NEW
YORK TIMES. 17:8, March 16, 1951.

1341 "Euthanasia for incurables in proposed Nazi
penal code," NEW YORK TIMES. 1:2,
October 8, 1933.

1342 "Four nurses get suspended sentences for
killing seven incurable patients unable
to flee from German invasion army," NEW
YORK TIMES. 4:6, May 30, 1942.

1343 "Frankfurt court acquits Drs. A. Albrich,
H. Bunke and K. Endruwert of complicity
in murder of mental patients during
Nazi mercy killing program," NEW YORK
TIMES. 11:1, May 24, 1967.

1344 "G. Bohne, charged with heading euthanasia
program, loses appeal in Argentina
against extradition to West Germany,"
NEW YORK TIMES. 4:1, August 28, 1966.

1345 "German church leaders helped form secret
public opinion against measures," NEW
YORK TIMES. 4:6, June 11, 1943.

1346 "German deputies defeat proposal that
physicians be allowed to cause painless
deaths in hopeless cases: views of
experts on problems of euthanasia,"
NEW YORK TIMES. III. 1:3, May 19, 1924.

1347 "Hamburg Health Department to let six
doctors who took part in mercy killings
of children under Nazis continue professional career," NEW YORK TIMES.
5:1, January 13, 1961.

1348 "Hefelmann charges Roman Catholic Church
was willing to tolerate mass mercy
killings," NEW YORK TIMES. 9:4, April
8, 1964.

1349 "Hefelmann details program to kill mentally and physically retarded; says
doctors were volunteers dedicated to
the idea of mercy deaths," NEW YORK
TIMES. 13:1, February 26, 1964.

1350 "Hefelmann details program says Drs. Catel,
Wentzler and Hinze made life or death
rulings," NEW YORK TIMES. 11:1, February 27, 1964.

1351 "Hefelmann testifies," NEW YORK TIMES.
5:1, February 25, 1964.

1352 "Hefelmann trial," NEW YORK TIMES. 2:5,
       February 20, 1964.

1353 "Hefelmann trial opens... reportedly sought
       mercy death for his own mother," NEW
       YORK TIMES. 5:2, February 19, 1964.

1354 "Hefelmann trial postponed indefinetely,"
       NEW YORK TIMES. 5:6, August 29, 1964.

1355 "Hefelmann trial recessed because of his
       health, to resume," NEW YORK TIMES.
       3:1, July 26, 1964.

1356 "Hesse state to try Drs. W. Heyde, G.
       Bohne and H. Hefelmann for mercy killing,"
       NEW YORK TIMES. 2:4, July 24, 1962.

1357 "Heyde pleads innocent," NEW YORK TIMES.
       42:6, November 15, 1959.

1358 "Intended victim's survival reveals six
       incurables killed in Orsay, France,
       hospital before German occupation; 3
       nurses held," NEW YORK TIMES. 3:2,
       October 1, 1940.

1359 "The issues of the Nuremburg Trial," by
       Wechsler. POLITICAL SCIENCE QUARTERLY.
       62:11-16, 1947.

1360 "Practice scorned by German confessional
       church," NEW YORK TIMES. 4:3, August
       4, 1944.

1361 "Two German doctors convicted for imple-
       menting Nazi euthanasia program," NEW
       YORK TIMES. 6:5, May 3, 1950.

1362 "Two German women medical attendants exe-
       cuted, Berlin, for killing 600 asylum
       patients under Nazi regime," NEW YORK
       TIMES. 14:6, January 15, 1947.

1363 "U. S. prosecutor J. McHaney tells Nurem-
      berg war crimes court that euthanasia,
      charged against four doctors, was ille-
      gal under Nazi German law," NEW YORK
      TIMES. 2:4, January 11, 1947.

AUTHOR INDEX

A

Abbott, W. M. 934, 1169
Abdou, H. I. 168
Adriant, J. 638
Agate, J. 954
Akenhurst, F. E. 565
Alexander, C. F. 591
Alexander, L. 1
Allred, V. C. 1017
Almeida, H. R. de. 1139
Alsop, S. 2, 198
Anderson, F. 1092
Anderson, S. 860, 1305
Anderson, W. F. 953
Anthony, G. N. 850, 1065
Aranez, J. B. 170
Archambault, P. R. 699
Armiger, B. 1129
Aubertin, E. 1253
Austin, A. 592
Ayd, J. F. Jr. 442

B

Badura, R. 172
Bailey, D. T. 424
Banks, A. L. 566, 1003
Barber, H. 517
Bard, B. 858, 1246
Barnes, E. W. 738
Barrere, I. 3
Barington, M. R. 4
Bavin, C. 717
Beach, K. H. 196
Beard, M. R. 930

Beart, J. E. 567
Beavan, J. 687
Beecher, H. K. 451, 499, 512, 1326
Beels, C. C. 5
Behnke, J. A. 537
Benjamin, H. 832
Benoliel, J. 6
Bergman, A. 501
Berkley, C. 754
Berry, F. B. 655
Biorck, G. 435, 682
Bizzarrini, G. 550
Blacker, C. P. 1330
Blackman, D. M. 164
Blackman, H. J. 620
Blaker, C. W. 483
Blanshard, P. 7
Blatch, H. S. 836
Blomquist, C. 8, 551, 680
Bloom, S. W. 9
Blume, N. R. 681
Boas, G. 1170
Bok, S. A. 10, 1012, 1317
Bonnet, E. F. 664
Bordet, F. 568
Bornemeler, W. C. 632
Bosh, G. 604
Bouquet, H. 184, 569
Bovel, J. 718
Bowen, J. M. 164
Box, H. R. 690
Brandli, W. R. 747
Brantner, J. 962
Brass, A. 847
Brightwell, D. R. 1273, 1310
Brill, A. A. 644
Brisard, C. 676

235

Ruppel, L. 732
Rusoen, S. 1007
Russell, 986

S

Sachett, W. W. Jr.,
534, 990, 991
Safar, P. 111
St. John-Stevas, N.
112
Sales, D. 639
Sanchez Valer, V.
114
Sanders, J. 1020
Scarlett, E. P. 932
Schaefer, J. 674,
1160
Schavelzon, J. 197
Schiff, A. F. 619
Schlaich, L. F. 115
Schmidt, G. 116
Schoenberg, B. 117
Schreuder, J. T. 721
Schwartz, W. 959
Schwitalla, A. M.
912
Scoffen, J. 955
Scott, W. N. 163
Senescu, R. 182
Serra, A. V. 584,
1140
Shambrom, E. 659
Sheerin, J. B. 924
Shepard, M. W.
759
Shideler, M. M. 768,
1134
Shields, D. 722
Shirer, W. L. 1333
Sholin, P. D. 533,
989
Silber, S. J. 536
Sillevaerts, C. 1335
Silverstein, M. E.
542

Silving, H. 1008
Simeons, A. T. W.
910
Simili, A. 585
Simonin, C. 625
Simons, S. M. 1059
Sinton, J. 723
Slater, E. 118, 635,
823
Smith, H. L. 119
Smith, S. L. H. 720,
724, 855
Snider, A. J. 1251
Soares, V. 120
Spencer, H. 121
Sperry, W. L. 903
Speigelman, M. 29
Sporken, P. 636
Stehlin, J. S. 196
Steinbauer, G. 122
Stern, A. I. 173
Stweart, H. L. 586
Streight, P. M. 1332
Strangberg, B. 124
Stratton, R. W. 982
Stureys, G. K. 693
Sullivan, J. V. 126,
127
Sullivan, M. T. 996
Sumner, F. B. 949
Sutherland, J. G. 79
Suzuki, M. 1036

T

Tedeschi, G. 1061
Thevenin, J. 128
Thompson, F. C. 129
Thompson, G. P. 1124
Thompson, P. W. 130
Thornstedt, H. 1011
Till-d'Aulnis de Bour-
iull, H von, 131
Tollemache, L. A. 840,
844

241